Anunnaki

Reptilians in the History of Humankind

(Autobiography and Explosive Revelations of a Human Anunnaki)

Manuel Rochon

Published By **Elena Holly**

Manuel Rochon

Anunnaki: Reptilians in the History of Humankind (Autobiography and Explosive Revelations of a Human Anunnaki)

ISBN 978-1-990373-98-5

No part of this guidebook shall be reproduced in any form without permission in writing from the publisher except in the case of brief quotations embodied in critical articles or reviews.

Legal & Disclaimer

The information contained in this book is not designed to replace or take the place of any form of medicine or professional medical advice. The information in this book has been provided for educational & entertainment purposes only.

The information contained in this book has been compiled from sources deemed reliable, and it is accurate to the best of the Author's knowledge; however, the Author cannot guarantee its accuracy and validity and cannot be held liable for any errors or omissions. Changes are periodically made to this book. You must consult your doctor or get professional medical advice before using any of the suggested remedies, techniques, or information in this book.

Table Of Contents

Chapter 1: What were they? Sumerians?

The Sumerians are mentioned in the archeological records that date back to around 4500 BCE. The Sumerians are located in modern-day Iraq (I was assigned from 2003 to Al Asaad in 2003-2004) This region a.k.a. Mesopotamia is long ago called "the cradle of civilization." Sumer was the name given to a number of city-states that was initially administered by priests. They were each centered around a temple or city which is now referred to as the " Ziggurat. " These ziggurats, which were committed for Anunnaki devotion, had built as layered and had flat-topped pyramids. The Anunnaki communities were thought as "servant-slave" populations dedicated to being devoted to the gods of the temple and the Anunnaki. In time, the priesthood's rule was replaced by kings.

Sumerian historical records are gleaned from fossils and archaeological evidencethe written record is made up of cuneiform tablets. According to reports, half a million tablets have been discovered However, only a few percentage were translated. Many of the information learned was derived from the translations of Babylonian archives; Sumer was considered "ancient" during Babylonian times.

Sumerians revered the Anunnaki gods who were believed to be heaven and earth's children; An, the sky god as well as Ki the goddess of earth. Most important among these was Enlil the god of Air. This god was passed on through people of the Akkadian, Babylonian, and Assyrian civilizations. It is the Epic of Gilgamesh, the tale of the king who was historical to Sumerian city-state Urek is a long-standing literary artifact from Sumerian civilization.

The above is the most popular "narrative" regarding the Anunnaki Others have come to various conclusions, based on archeological evidence, an analysis of

Sumerian mythology, as well as transcriptions of ancient cuneiform tablets.

The Flipside of the Annunaki Story

The author Michael Cremo ("Forbidden Archaeology") has been researching the past of archaeology over the past 40+ years and has documented findings which have not been included in the mainstream archaeology of academics and findings that could alter the accepted mythology of the origins of humans.

Cremo together with authors Zecharia Sitchin Erich von Daniken (author, "Chariots of the Gods") along with author and researcher Michael Tellinger, and several others, offers compelling evidence to suggest that the Anunnaki were actually an off-world entity posing in the form of "gods." This theory further asserts that the "sky" gods genetically engineered humans into a slave race that could explain weaknesses in the evolution narrative. This theory gave rise to"the "ancient astronaut" hypothesis asserting that alien creatures have been pretending to be gods to shape human behavior throughout the many millennia.

A lot of people believe that the Annunaki took huge amounts of gold through human labour This is believed to come from the numerous excavations of ancient mining tunnels located in South Africa, as well as links and relics back to Sumerians. "No one knows why they wanted gold, no one knows how much was taken," told Tellinger. The Annunaki established the concept of money, finance and debt to the human society.

An idea that they were derived out of "Nibiru," a.k.a. "Planet X" has been included in alternate Anunnaki stories, and also the possibility of gods who are from another world bringing technological advancements that explain advanced megastructures, such as the pyramids and Stonehenge. Artifacts found in strange places and tools are a part of these assumptions. These Sumerians are also well-known for their advanced mathematical and astronomical knowledge that is believed to have come through the Annunaki.

Annunaki god Enki

Although not any list that are part of the Annunaki pantheon are available however, we know that every Sumerian city-state has their particular Annunaki god/overseer, chosen by an elder Annunaki Marduk.

A few, possibly inspired to some extent by Theosophical Society founder Helena Blavatsky's book "The Secret Doctrine," affirm that Annunaki are Annunaki were a reptilian species which is still alive and is deeply entangled in the human world. In the book, Blavatsky spoke of "dragon men" who influenced the forgotten Lemurian civilization.

David Icke has been on the disclosure/conspiracy lecture circuit since

1999 -- he accurately reported that U.K. TV and radio star Jimmy Savile was a rampant pedophile, proven true after Savile's death in 2011.

Icke believes that the false Anunnaki gods are still manipulating humans from the thrones of power as well as financial control across the world. The author explains how these gods don't just kill humans, they take advantage of fear and collective anxiety. Icke demands a break from the mainstream media as well as Orwellian influence that creates anxiety and fear which creates an overall experience of hypnosis.

There are many who agree with Icke's opinion. Surprisingly it appears as a totally absurd theory. However, if you follow the breadcrumbs to discover an intriguing story that spans from the beginning of time to today as well as make your own conclusion.

Anunnaki Bible

(Genesis) IN THE BEGINNING

4600,000,000 years B.C. (i.e. prior to Christ (or in the Christian (i.e. before Christ, or the Christian) (i.e. before Christ, or the Christian era) Earth begins to form. This is the widely acknowledged date for the beginning of the history of Earth. The oldest rock found on Earth zircon crystals are believed to date back 4200 million years ago.

Zecharia Sitchin has suggested theories about the birth of the Earth that is based on Sumerian epics about creation, such as one called Enuma Elish. The epics mention that the planets were described as gods and were given names like gods from the Anunnaki.

3,500,000,000 to 600,000,000 ~ The Precambrian Era.

3420,000,000 to 31335,000,000 monocelled organisms make their way into the oceans around the Earth.

600,000,000 to 500,000,000 ~ The Paleozoic Era; Cambrian Period. 500,000,000 to

425,000,000 ~ The Paleozoic Era; Ordovician Period.

425,000,000 to 405,000,000 ~ The Paleozoic Era; Silurian Period.

405,000,000 to 345,000,000 ~ The Paleozoic Era; Devonian Period.

345,000,000 to 280,000,000 ~ The Paleozoic Era; Carboniferous Period.

280,000,000 to 220,000,000 ~ The Paleozoic Era; Permian Period.

220,000,000 to 181,000,000 ~ The Mesozoic Era; Triassic Period. This was the time of dinosaurs.

200 million The continent Pangea begins to divide into a northern continental, Laurasia, and a southern continent known as Gondwana.

181,000,000 to 135,000,000 ~ The Mesozoic Era; Jurassic Period. Animals first appear on Earth at this point in time However, they don't thrive because of the power of dinosaurs.

135,000,000 to 65,000,000 ~ The Mesozoic Era; Cretaceous Period.

65,000,000 Laurasia 65,000,000 Laurasia Gondwana are beginning to break up into smaller parts, and ultimately will form the current continents.

65,000,000 dinosaurs - The dinosaurs went extinct all over the world.

65,000,000 to 54,000,000 ~ The Cenozoic Era; Tertiary Period; Paleocene Epoch.

54,000,000 to 36,000,000 ~ The Cenozoic Era; Tertiary Period; Eocene Epoch.

36,000,000 to 25,000,000 ~ The Cenozoic Era; Tertiary Period; Oligocene Epoch.

30,000,000 - 25,000,000 species resembling apes are seen on Earth in the Oligocene Era.

25,000,000 to 5,000,000 ~ The Cenozoic Era; Tertiary Period; Miocene Epoch.

14,000,000 Hominids or man-like Apes, first appear on Earth as a result of evolution.

11,000,000. First appearance of the apes that can be classed in the category of Homo in Earth.

5,000,000 to 1,000,000 ~ The Cenozoic Era; Tertiary Period; Pliocene Epoch.

3,750,000-3,000,000 Australopithecus afarensis live on Earth. The creatures, despite having extremely ape-like heads, also had much more human-like bodies. In Laetoli in Tanzania the fossilized footprints of been found on two humans and a child. They reveal that they were walking with two legs. The stones on which the footprints are found have been traced at 3,750,000 B.C. The skeleton that was discovered by Don Johanson and Tom Gray in Hadar located in Ethiopia, Africa, which they identified as Lucy was part of this group. It is believed to date back to 3,000,000 B.C. (3,500,000 according to certain experts). Some anthropologists have dated the Australopithecines older than that, implying that they were between 4 and 5 million years ago.

3,000,000 - 2,000,000 Australopithecus africanus are found on the Earth.

2,800,000 Australopithecus Afarensis was gone out of fossil records by the time this was written.

2,000,000 - 1,750,000 Homo Habilis Australopithecus boisei, and Australopithecus Rebustus are all found on the Earth.

Between 2,000,000 and 40,000 of beings that can be categorized as Homo erectus are found on Earth. (Some experts have estimated the date of Homo sexually active as long to 3,000,000.) It is believed that they originated from Homo hominis. Between 750,000 and 1,000,000 years ago, these creatures were spread out across Africa into Europe in Europe and Asia. At 700,000 just Homo erectus was a living thing on the Earth in accordance with the archaeological evidence.

1,000,000 to 11,000 ~ The Cenozoic Era; Quaternary Period; Pleistocene Epoch.

1,000,000 Australopithecus boisei as well as Australopithecus Rebustus vanish from fossil records by this point. Homo habilis, which was the very first specimen of the Homo Genus, is continuing to exist.

800,000 - The time period referred to as the Old Stone Age begins.

600,000 to 550,000 ~ First Ice Age.

480,000 to 430,000 ~ Second Ice Age.

In the spirit of Mr. Sitchin The wars of Gods and Men and The Lost book of Enki, I've created this Timeline in order to document the Anunnaki incidents.

500 million years ago The world Nibiru begins to suffer a degrading of the atmosphere. However, not just the atmospheric conditions were deteriorating and the kingship of Nephilim was in turmoil which would ultimately lead to the expansion of the Nephilim on Earth. In the Nephilim custom it was the Beginning. There followed an era known as the Prior Times.

The Prior Times was a time with a great deal of war and conflict. Then, peace was announced in which it was agreed that to bring about peace, a chief from north be married to a female chosen from the south. Then, their child would then become the chief of a united Nibiru.

The very first Nephilim King to be named after peace was made was AN. The appointement by AN to the throne of Nibiru along with his wife AN.TU signified the conclusion of the Prior Times and the beginning of the Olden Times.

Nibiru's rule, later, passed to those who descend on AN, (i.e. The Celestial One).

AN was succeeded in reign of the king by AN.KI (i.e. By AN A Solid Foundation), son of AN and AN.TU (i.e. the leader of the Spouse of AN).

AN.KI passed away without an heir as his rule was succeeded by his elder brother AN.IB (i.e. the Middle One who is the AN's Son).By his wife NIN.IB (i.e. the Lady of IB), AN.IB bore one son named AN.SHAR.GAL (i.e. AN's Prince Who Is Greatest Of Princes).

AN.SHAR.GAL's partner was KI.SHAR.GAL who she was born AN.SHAR.

AN.SHAR got married to KI.SHAR.

AN.SHAR's next of kin was the son EN.SHAR (i.e. Lordly Master of The Shar) and his wife was referred to as NIN.SHAR.

They were the parents of DU.URU (i.e. In the Dwelling Place Fashioned) whom he was his choice for wife DA.URU (i.e. She Who Is By My Side).

DA.URU wasn't of the royal family, but was an acquaintance of DU.URU's childhood. The couple never had no children, instead DA.URU was her foster son one of the children she found in the palace gates.

DA.URU's violation of the law of succession caused the court to go in confusion.

Called LAHMA (i.e. Dryness) The child later was crowned king. He married LAHAMA.

The time of the reign of AN.SHAR the eruptions of volcanoes which for so long maintained the earth's atmosphere did not have the same activity like they were they were before. In the end, the shield that protects the air began to break. The shattered atmospheric canopy went on throughout EN.SHAR's and DU.URU's dominions and even to the reign of LAHMA. Two options were suggested:

One was to shoot Weapons of Terror into the volcanoes, making them active and active

Chapter 2: Another was to repair the crack with gold dust that had been pulverized

LAHMA was unable to decide on what method to use in order to repair the deterioration of the atmospheric conditions of Nibiru. The crisis was becoming increasingly desperate. By taking advantage of the crisis it was the time to rouse people into rebellion

ALALU is an heir to the princehood, descends on AN.SHAR.GAL via the daughter ALAM (whose mom was actually concubine). ALALU considered that the throne was legitimately his through the rules of succession.

ALALU entered the palace. The consequence of a clash between the two men, LAHMA was taken away from the palace's tower and was thrown to the ground. He died. ALALU declared himself King.

ANU was present at a meeting that was part of The Seven Who Judge and declared ANU, and not ALALU ANU, was the proper the ruler of Nibiru. ANU traces his lineage an even more precise line than ALULU and, therefore, claimed to the title of king.

ANU descends from AN through AN.IB Then through an son through AN.IB's wedding to the daughter EN.URU The oldest brother from AN as well as AN.TU.

EN.URU became a wife to with his half-sister NIN.URU and they had a child to EN.AMA. One child of EN.AMA was the prince named ANU.

The Seven Who Judge called for ALALU as a candidate, and then he presented an appeal to ANU. The king, ALALU, would retain the throne for as long as he lived and ANU will retain the succession to the throne, and his children could become kings at a later date.

ANU was acquiescent to the idea after which he became the cup bearer of ALALU.

He was however not content with the situation, and was forced to work for ALALU even though he felt that it was his right to be the the king.

Then, after nine Shars (i.e. Nibiru year, which is nine circuits complete around the Sun), ANU rose to the challenge of ALALU. They fought and ANU won. ANU was declared the king and while he was transported to the palace ALALU fled to safety.

He snatched a spaceship, and sped to the other side of Nibiru.

The destination of his journey was Ki (i.e. Earth). While he was not planning to however, he found on Earth the rare metal gold, that can be used for repairing the rifts in Nibiru's atmosphere.

Earth was also known as the "seventh planet" to the Nephilim of Nibiru due to the fact that it was recorded from the outer areas of the Solar System (i.e. 1. Gaga/Pluto

~ 2. Ea/Neptune ~ 3. Anu/Uranus ~ 4. Anshar/Saturn ~ 5. Kishar/Jupiter ~ 6. Lahmu/Mars ~ 7. Ki/Earth ~ 8. Lahamu/Venus ~ 9. Mummu/Mercury

445,000 BC Approximately five Earth-years (i.e. approximately one-third Nibiru years) following ALALU's escape travel to Nibiru towards Earth, ANU authorizes his son, E.A (i.e. the one who is home to water) to go on a journey with an entire group of fifty Nephilim towards the "seventh planet' to confirm that the claims of ALALU are true and accurate.

The Nephilim that have travelled from the planet they call home, Nibiru, to the seventh planet are known as, AN.UNNA.KI (i.e. Those Who From Heaven To Earth Came Down)

In the first six days following their arrival after landing, the town is established in Eridu (i.e. home In The Faraway, or Earth Station 1), located in the area they named the Edin was established by E.A and his team.

The extraction of gold from waters starts, even although the amount is small, Nibiru demands delivery.

Abgal is a pilot who decides to use the spacecraft of ALALU on his journey back to Nibiru. The weapons that are forbidden within the craft. E.A Abgal and E.A. remove the weapon of terror, and put them in a cave in Earth. The Nibiruians take note of even the tiny gold-based delivery. Testing of the use of gold for an atmospheric shield are successful.

The Hebrew belief in the 6 days of creation could originate from the earlier documented Sumerian report of the landing of the Anunnaki as well as their establishment at Eridu. This account reveals that particular jobs were completed on certain days, for instance the study and recording of plants, herbs and plants during the 3rd day as well as the recording and investigation of the various creatures that wandered or moved during the sixth day. E.A announced 7th day of the week would be a rest day.

It is believed that the Sumerian phrase, E.DIN, translates as"Home of the Righteous. It was within E.DIN where the city, E.RI.DU was created. Its name is translated into many languages around the globe, such as Erde which is German, Erthe in Middle English, Ertz in Kurdish Eretz in Kurdish, and Eretz as in Hebrew. Eretz has also become the term that English natives use to refer to Earth.

The location where E.DIN was founded was located in the region that was drained by Tigris as well as the Euphrates rivers. It was also the site that became known as Mesopotamia. The two peaks of the mountain referred to as Arrata or Ararat served to serve as a landing point for Nephilim's spacecraft.

440,000 BC. The emergence of more Nephilim will require that the settlement on Earth increase. In this time EN.LIL and then his father ANU go between Nibiru towards Earth in order to find out if gold retrieval is possible to increase due to the fact that what was delivered to Nibiru does not suffice to fix any of the holes in Nibiru's atmospheric.

The gold that had been discovered thus far was from the sea. It was in an already well-refined state, and was ready for use (albeit following the process of pulverization). E.A. explored the continents of the Earth through a "sky chamber', in search of gold ore-bearing rocks. The find was substantial of gold ore in the region of Abzu (i.e. the southern/lower/nether region), which corresponds to the present-day region of southern Africa along the Zambezi River.

On Nibiru On Nibiru, the Nephilim began to get impatient about the gold they desperately needed.

EN.LIL was commanded by his father ANU in order to visit the seventh world to discover the reason behind E.A's discovered gold in veins of Earth as well as his idea to mine it had never ever been implemented. In Earth, E.A explained to his younger brother the challenges that come with mining gold out of the rock. The two also debated the issue regarding who would be the one to oversee mining activities and who will be the commander of for the Eridu settlement. They urged their fathers to visit the Earth to settle the issues.

ANU was discovered on Earth and was notified by E.A. regarding his findings. Then, ANU traveled across Abzu(south Africa) to inspect the gold-bearing mineral. It was decided who should be in charge of the mining operations was raised in the meeting, and ANU recommended that he, E.A. and EN.LIL could draw lots in order to determine who will be the king for The Home In The Faraway, the gold mining operation within Abzu, the gold mining operations in Abzu or even the reign of Nibiru.

The draw of the lot was the result of ANU staying as the king of Nibiru. EN.LIL was later to be The Lord of the Command of Eridu and further settlements were added in the Edin. E.A would become EN.KI (i.e. the Master of Earth).

For the purpose of overseeing the gold mining process in the Abzu.EN.KI constructed his home there. We now are calling it Great Zimbabwe.

ALALU was not included in the draw of the lotteries This angered the ALALU. He asked ANU to a new wrestling bout to protect his honour. ANU was in agreement and the two teams took on a fight and ANU defeating ALALU again. However, as ANU lifted his feet away from the body of ALALU ANU, ALALU climbed up, and slashed ANU's torso.

ANU was able to survive and then returned to Nibiru for healing. ALALU was exiled by the tribunal in The Seven Who Judge to a living on a surface of Lahma(Mars) His grandson AN.ZU chooses to remain with his grandfather and live on Mars.

415,000 BC NIN.HUR.SAG traverses between Nibiru through the seventh planet, Earth. As the Chief Medical Officer the mission is to attend to health complaints made by people called the Anunnaki who live on Earth.Stopping off on Mars she discovers ALALU deceased. A carved rock, which resembles ALALU.s face is used as an tomb.AN.ZU ALALU's grandchild is appointed the commander of the Waystation located on Mars.

NIN.HUR.SAG is on Earth with information about EN.LIL from their son who is not yet married Ninurta.

400 000 BC - A cluster with eight cities is created and then completed in E.DIN the

city of Nippur (also known as Nibru-ki) (i.e. The Bond Heaven-Earth) is now an Mission Control Center. The total number of Nibiruians in Earth exceed 600. Another 300 known as IGI.GI provide shuttlecraft services and the orbiting station.

At the time of 360,000BC Sippar was erected to be a spaceport. Other cities within the complex are:

* Shuruppak is an medical center to facilitate the utilization of Ninhursag

* Bad-Tibira founded as an industrial hub to smelt and refining the gold mined from Abzu. Abzu

* Laarsa and Lagash are beacon cities for spacecraft that are about to enter the area.

320,000 BC Imprisoned for the act of date-raped Sud. EN.LIL discovers the secret

weapoms. Sud turns into EN.LIL,s wife NIN.LIL and bears the son(Nannar) NIN.MAH who joins EN.KI and EN.KI in Africa and

27

bears daughters. NIN.KI, EN.KI,s spouse, comes together with the son of their marriage, MAR.DUK. Clans are born on Earth in the form of EN.KI and EN.LIL create additional sons.

Ores arrive via ships coming from Africa and the finished metal is shipped to Baalbek.

Chapter 3: orbiters that are manned by IGI.GI.

They were then transferred to spaceships that arrived regularly from Nibiru. 300,000 BC Then, around the fortieth of the shar (i.e. 3600 years) following the arrival of the Nephilim in Earth The Anunnaki that had been given the task of mining gold mines in Abzu(south Africa) stage a revolt.

In gaining the trust of the Igigi Alalu's grandson AN.ZU seeks to establish a supreme power over Earth. The Enlilites win the War of the Olden Gods.

EN.KI and NIN.HUR.SAG try to find the possibility of taking on the burdensome work of the Anunnaki.After working for more than forty "periods of time' and then the Anunnaki revolted and demanded relief. They came to EN.LIL asking for relief but he refused to listen to their pleas and so they contacted ANU to offer relief. EN.KI is always the character of Anunnaki, suggested the Lullu (i.e. the primitive worker also known as Lullu Amelu) Lullu Amelu) was created in order to carry the burden of. The Lullu Amelu was an ancient being that existed on Earth that was similar to Anunnaki which could be improved by an image from the Anunnaki. In the end, Enlil refuses to accept and screams Creation is the work of God of all Beginning Our image only to the existing being Ninmah says. In desperate need of gold, the leaders approve of an inhumane worker who will replace the labor that is the Anunnaki.

EN.KI seeks to track down the wild, primitive man who wanders around the Abzu. EN.KI discovers and captures a few of the wild people along with his son NINGISHZIDDA performs tests which reveal they're akin to Nephilim.

After many failures, method by which mankind was created - Homo sapiens sapiens (i.e. the Lullu one, also known as the one that has mixed blood') was created, was through genetically altering Homo Erectus species that lived on the Earth prior to the advent from the Anunnaki. However, rather than the 'creation' of most strict sense The method that EN.KI and NIN.HUR.SAG together with NINGISHZIDDA and NINGISHZIDDA brought Adamu into existence Adamu to existence was through introducing with the Nephilim DNA into beings who already existed on Earth which was the ancient Homo Erectus.

The species that populated Earth before the advent of the Nephilim could have come from the home planet of Nibiru, the home planet of Nephilim, Nibiru, and ended up onto Earth as it collided into Nibiru as well as its moons. So, all the living species, like the 'caveman and the 'caveman' Homo erectus, may have genetically compatible with Nibiru's life varieties that are found on Nibiru. The simplest way to describe it is the sperm/semen of EN.KI (Father) came to be put into the eggs of an Homo erectus female through the method known as cross-fertilization. The fertilized egg, called the embryo was later inserted in NIN.KI's, EN.KI's wife's womb in which it was fed by the blood of her and developed to become a human being.

EN.KI has named him Adamu. NIN.KI is then able to help EN.KI create an earthling female, and they give her the name Ti-Amat. The incident occurred in the E.DIN manufacturing facility.

Adamu Adamu was the very first Human The first human weren't able to reproduce thus more humans were created by the Birth Goddesses. Birth goddess was viewed as a snub by the people of Nibiru therefore another genetic modification was created by

NINGISHZIDDA used the essence of life (dna) of EN.KI"s the rib that was placed in the male workers as well as the dna of the female rib anunnaki was injected into the female human, so Human workers were able to produce offspring and reproduce via themselves..the story of the rib is in the Bible. Following the news, EN.LIL directed that the Humans quit the E.DIN and sent to Abzu. Abzu mining of gold immediately. Abzu Adamu and Ti-Amat have twins and children. two daughters and a son. There are many other children.

Homo sapiens sapiens first appear from the Earth. Many anthropologists believe Homo sapiens sapiens arose from Homo erectus. However, the link has not ever been proved. The site of Zhoukoudian in close proximity to Peking, China, a settlement that was part of Homo sapiens sapiens was equipped with an open hearth where the residents could heat themselves. The same hearth was discovered in the Terra Amata site on the Mediterranean coastline of France and is believed to date back to around 300,000 B.C. The evidence of cooperative or communal actions suggest that a kind of language existed during the time of this. In the year 200,000, it was thought that there was there was no Homo Erectus was still in existence.

200 000 BC - Life in Earth is able to regress during an era of glaciation. Humans multiply and assume the work in the ABZU mining gold, as well as serve as servants to the Anunnaki of the Abzu as well as the E.DIN

EN.LIL's grandkids, twins Utu and Innana have been born. Couples from the Anunnaki tribe also have offspring here on Earth.

The effects of climate change cause difficulties in Earth as well as Mars as the orbit of Nibirus nears completion. can be followed by major changes.

EN.KI and Marduk investigate the moon and finding it unhospitable. EN.KI decides on the constellations as well as the celestial clock. A bit irritated about his own destiny EN.KI assures supremacy to Marduk however Anu will hand over the spaceport's new location to Utu and not Marduk.

110,200-56,200 BC While looking at the Humans that he created, EN.KI noticed two of the human females bathing in the stream within the E.DIN, EN.KI had his approach to both.

They were able to give birth to two children both males as well as a female.

Enki's children.who were half-brothers and sister. EN.KI gave them the names ADAPA and TI.TI and would eventually be referred to as Eve. One of the unique aspects with ADAPA and TI.TI / ADAM and TI.TI or EVE was the fact that they were cross-bred, and despite having a genetic connection to EN.KI as well as humans could reproduce in their own.

EN.KI brings his kids to the gardens located in E.DIN in order to learn and be covered in the same way as Nephilim. Royal Human Bloodline begins.

ADAPA, the Adama, or 'First Of A Kind' (i.e. Civilized Man) more accurately it was the very first of its kind. This first human being to be civilized would be known in the future and also by the spiritual ancestors of the Sumerians and the Judeo-Christians also known as Adam. The theory suggests that Adam existed between of the 93rd and the 108th Shar prior to the emergence of the Nephilim on Earth around 445,000 years ago. This would be roughly 101,000 years ago to the year 56200 BC. Human genetics suggests the date being sixty thousand years in the past.

ADAPA as just a child was transported into Nibiru through his Nephilim family, DU.MU.ZI and NINGISHZIDDA, EN.KI,s others sons, who were who were then presented to ANU. When he left Earth, EN.KI gave to NINGISHZIDDA an electronic tablet that contained the details of ADAPA's creation by his life force, as well as the idea that ADAPA must be prohibited from drinking or eating Nibiru foods, in order to provide him, as well as his heirs, the possibility of living that was based on Nibiru shar cycles that last three years equal to Earth years.

ANU offered ADAPA in order to assist him in his return back to Earth and the seeds with which the cultivation of grains can be made as well as the vitality of the sheep, from which domestic cattle could be reared.

ADAPA and ADAPA ADAM and TI.TI and EVE were married

EVE got pregnant and had twins born The first son was named KA.IN..

and another one is HEVEL as well as the one titled HEVEL ABAEL.

KA.IN (i.e. He Who Is In The Field The Food Plants) with the help of NINURTA was instructed on reaping and sowing of the cereal grains that Nephilim offered to Adapa.

His younger brother, ABAEL (i.e. He of the Watered Meadows), by the direction of

MARDUK was trained by MARDUK to birth and raise of animals.

In the course of a few years, following the development of the crops through KA.IN as well as the rearing of sheep through ABAEL They and the results of their work were handed over before EN.LIL along with ENKI.

Both sons of earth were honored by EN.LIL however, only ABAEL got praise from EN.KI.ABAEL exclaimed about EN.KI's praises to KA.IN however, which caused a fury to KA.IN. They argued among the other, and then one day after KA.IN took his family to the fields of ABAEL's, he was enraged ABAEL. He yelled at KA.IN to leave. They began fighting until anger was so intense within KA.IN that he began to raise an object and hurled it into the head of his brother ABAEL.

The vitality of ABAEL was reflected in his body.

KA.IN upon realizing he'd done something wrong, stood by the body of his brother and began to cry.

In the event that EN.KI was informed about the events that had occurred, and of the loss of ADAPA's son who was MAR.DUK's pupil, EN.KI became very enraged and cursed KA.IN.

EN.KI demonstrated to ADAPA the proper way to interment his son ABAEL in the manner that the Nephilim are buried. When he was brought before the group from The Seven Who Judge, it was recommended by MAR.DUK to demand that KA.IN be executed. However, EN.KI was able to convince EN.KI to have him removed from the E.DIN. The death penalty could eliminate an avenue to further earthling procreation, and would the growth.

EN.KI's idea of exile was accepted in The Seven Who Judge, and that is why KA.IN could remain living, but was forever exiled from E.DIN into in the Land of Wandering.

To signify those who came to meet KA.IN or his family members, the essence of his existence was changed to ensure that his family and he were not allowed to have an eyebrow on their face. The third child that was born in ADAPA's family and TI.TI was called SAT.NAAL SATI/SETH (i.e. He Who Life Binds Again). The birth occurred in the 95th year since the appearance of the Nephilim on Earth in the time of 103,000 BC.

ADAPA and TITI had sixty more children. Thirty sons and 30 daughters.

In the 97th shar of the appearance of the Nephilim on Earth (i.e. 95,800 B.C.E.), SATI and his partner, AZURA, gave birth to a son ENSHI (i.e. Master Of Humanity). An understanding of the rituals that are associated with the Anunnaki was first discovered by ENSHI whom was also known by the Hebrew custom as Enosh.

The 98th Shar following the appearance of the Nephilim on Earth (i.e. 92,200 B.C.E.) Enshi as well as his wife, his sister NOAM was a mother to an infant son named KUNIN (i.e. He Of The Kilns). KUNIN was trained in the art of refining and melting to refine the ore of gold.

The 99th Shar following the arrival of the Nephilim on Earth (i.e. 88,600 B.C.E.) A boy was born by KUNIN and his partner as well as his half sister MUALIT. The baby was christened MALALU (i.e. He Who Plays). MALALU was also known by the Hebrew custom as Mahalalel.

On the 100th day from the time of the first appearance of the Nephilim in Earth (i.e. 85,000 B.C.E.), MALALU and his partner, DUNNA, gave birth to a son named IRID (i.e. He Of The Sweet Waters). IRID was popular by the Hebrew custom as Jared.

IRID was married to, BARAKA, the daughter of his father's brother and was married in the 102nd shar following the appearance of the Nephilim on Earth (i.e. 77,800 B.C.E.) A son was born to the couple. The name of the son was ENKI.ME (i.e. By ENKI ME Understanding). The ME contained miniature objects encoding with all the details of Nephilim research and understanding. EN.KI was attracted to ENKI.ME as he taught his a few facts about Nibiru as well as the stars, which previously he imparted to ADAPA the son of ENKI. MAR.DUK was the one who took ENKI.ME to space on his journeys and landed on the Moon and also to Lahmu and Mars. According to the Hebrew culture, ENKI.ME is referred to as Enoch.

In the 104th shar of the appearance of the Nephilim on Earth (i.e. 70,600 B.C.E.), ENKI.ME and his wife, half-sister EDINNI and EDINNI gave birth to three sons: MATUSHAL (i.e. Who By The Bright Waters Raised), RAGIM, and GAIDAD. MATUSHAL was identified by the Hebrew traditions as Methuselah.

The family of MATUSHAL and his partner, EDNAT, was born to a son named LU.MACH (i.e. Mighty Man) often known as Ubartutu. In Hebrew custom, LU.MACH was known by the title of Lamech. The circumstances on Earth got more severe, since workers for the Anunnaki the LU-MACH needed to enforce strict rations for the population. And at the same period, ADAPA became ill.

ADAPA was quite old, and his days were drawing to the ending. ADAPA pleaded with all his sons to listen to his last words before his death which included his beleaguered son KA.IN.

KA.IN was found in a faraway place when Ninurta was looking for him and he discovered him using an aircraft.

The beardless KA.IN along with his brother SATI were able to visit ADAPA at the end of his life.

ADAPA informed KA.IN that for the murder of your brother AB.EL the right to birth as a the king would be taken away however, from your seed there will be seven nations. Even if for murdering your brother through a stone, bring about the end of your life. SA.TI was blessed to be ADAPA's successor.

ADAPA requested that all of his children and grandchildren visit him to say goodbye and also to be buried at the place of his birth by the river.

Then, after ADAPA was gone, KA.IN and Sati put his body into the cloth, and then buried him in a cave near the river.

At the time that ADAPA was laid to rest, KA.IN returned to his place of his wandering. the distant place KA.IN was a father to daughters and sons and as he began to build the city of their dreams, his life was cut short with a stone that fell.

Mankind expands, and ADAPA's bloodline is used as Royalty. In defiance of ENLIL

Marduk, to a female Earthling. As cosmic disturbances and climate change influence Mars and the IGI.GI descend into Earth and seek wives to their own from Earthlings too.

Between 100,000 and 30,000 beings that are classified as Homo sapiens Neanderthalensis (i.e. Neandertals) are found on Earth. The evolution of Neandertal man could have come due to an adaptation to a harsh climate. There is evidence that animals' bones as well as stone tools found in graves of Neandertals provide evidence of the existence of an afterlife that would require such items. Skeletal remains show evidence of previously treated wounds, suggesting that the injured Neandertal was taken care of by family members or the community. The Neandertals suddenly vanished about 30000 B.C.

100,000 to 30,000 years ago Anunnaki males start to mat to female Earthlings. Based on the Hebrew Bible (Genesis:

chapter six, verse 4,), "the sons of God came in unto the daughters of men."

The kids born out of the matings between Anunnaki earthlings of males and females are often called the Naphidem (also known as Watchers) and they were the ones that the notion that there were angels was first conceived. The Greek term angelos is the word from where the English term 'angel' comes taken, refers to a "messenger," instead of the supernatural, ethereal being. The Naphidem who were partially descendent from the Nephilim and the Nephilim, started to assert supremacy over earthling males who in the earliest texts are described as the Eljo. The tension that came to be a reality between the Nephidems and the Eljo ultimately exploded into a conflict, where the Eljo race almost disappeared. According to the Sitchin's study, the term Nephilim roots mean to be thrown down or to fall. The title of the race that originated from Nibiru was Nephilim. Anunnaki, and iggi are merely ranks from the Nephilim. 77,000 bc. Shuruppak is a city in the region of Shuruppak is administered by Ubartutu who was a descendant from Adapa. The name he is given to him is Lamech being the father of Utnapishtim or Ziusudra (aka Noah). The truth is that Ubartutu and Lamech wasn't the father in biological form of Utnapishtim or Ziusudra and Noah As will be revealed in the following.

75,000-25,000 BC Homo sapiens sapiens are the inhabitants of Earth. Differently referred to as Cro Magnon, at the time they are here, they've almost completely replaced Neanderthals as the most dominant race of humans around 40 000 years ago.

49,000 BC ZIUSUDRA 49,000 bc ZIUSUDRA UTNAPISHTIM 4.9.19.19. NOAH has been born. He is the child of EN.KI and an earthling Batanash who is also the wife and niece of Lu-Mach/ Lamech. The identity of his father's birth is hidden, and he's treated as if he were Lu-Mach's son. The baby is the first who was born in the United States with blue eyes as well as dark hair..And the way he appeared was more like the Anunnaki than anyone else and is named his name as Ziusudra (i.e. He Of Long Bright Life Days), and Utnapishtim (i.e. Refrain) since it was believed that his fate was to bring to Earth relief from the suffering. He was referred to as Noah according to the Hebrew custom. ZIUSUDRA was married to EMZARA and together there were three sons born.

4000 bc Homo erectus has been discovered in only specific places, such as Java.

38,000 BC = EN.LIL gets annoyed by the growth of humans, as well as their appetites for food. The climate had even changed to become dry and harsh. EN.LIL is convinced that the difficulties that earthlings as well as the Anunnaki as well is directly due to the untamed promiscuity of earthlings, as well as the plans to cause their demise. The plan of the lord is for Anunnaki to abandon the Earth and in masse and then return to

Nibiru with the earthlings alone to decide their destiny. The reason for this is in part because EN.LIL, EN.KI, NIN.HUR.SAG as well as the other genuine Anunnaki and Nephilim beings notice they age faster on Earth and not so on Nibiru.

The lengthy circuit, also known as an orbit of Nibiru in the solar system, creating a single calendar year for those living in Nibiru (i.e. one shar) was equivalent to 3600 Earth years. For as long as Nephilim remain at Earth and traveled on their shorter circular orbit around the sun their lives were speeded up. Furthermore, while the Nephilim lived on Nibiru the Nephilim were able to drink a liquid which allowed them to live for long but the sought-after elixir not available when they were on Earth which meant that the lives of their fellow Nephilim were swiftly reaching their end.

EN.LIL, EN.KI and NIN.HUR.SAG talked about going back to Nibiru in order to avoid their impending death in Earth However, GALZU declaring that GALZU was an emissary from ANU and arrived in the form of a sealed tablet of Nibiru's king. Nibiru. The message GALZU gave to the ANU's kids was that they could never going to be able to return to Nibiru. Scientists and priests from Nibiru were of the opinion that allowing returning to the planet they call home could almost certainly mean that they would die because of the negative consequences of being on the planet Earth for so many years.

Between 30,000 and 20,000 years ago Humanity's race is divided into four distinct racial groupings:

1.) Caucasoids - - present-day Europeans as well as Indians as well as Hamites and Semites

2.) Mongoloids Present-day Asians as well as American Indians

3.) Australoids The present-day Australian Aboriginals

4.) Negroids

17,000-9500 B.C. Some animals, including dogs and sheep are domesticated, possibly as an animal source for food. They were then followed by the horned pigs and goats and non-horned cattle.

13,000 BC. 13,000 bc Anunnaki begin to realize that the next moment that Nibiru is close to the Earth the massive tide wave could be created.

ANU issued a second message to his sons and daughter that the shifts in climate and the other changes similar to those that they observed on Earth are caused by the tension that was created through the approach of Nibiru to Earth. Nibiru's Nephilim who resided on Nibiru were able to predict that the transit of the two planets would cause an influx of water on Earth because the glaciers that covered large portions of the poles would become warmer and raise the depth of the oceans. ANU advised his students to get into space chariots when the transit of the two planets took place in order to travel through the happenings expected to take place.

EN.LIL forced the remainder of the Anunnaki that they would keep information about the natural catastrophe that was coming from earthlings, in order for them to not be demolished. However, EN.KI was unable the thought of seeing his own creations lost, so he worked to protect a handful of his creations. He didn't speak directly about the upcoming flooding to Ziusudra and Noah instead, but towards wall of reed house that Ziusudra was a resident. In the course of his conversation Ziusudra was able to hear the words EN.

Chapter 4: 12,000 BC The Deluge is sweeping across the Earth

In the moment that Nibiru was moving towards Earth as it approached Earth, the Earth was shaking as lightning flashed across the sky. The force generated by gravity fields from both planets brought massive destruction on the atmospheres of both planets. However, the effects were more severe on Earth because of the bigger magnitude of Nibiru. The Anunnaki embarked on their airships, and was lifted up in the sky above Earth at which point they were able to observe the Deluge.

While they watched, the glaciers on the south pole began to break apart. Massive slabs of ice fell towards the ocean, at first increasing the height of the ocean a little. But then the massive mass of the southern glacier broke into pieces and fell into the sea creating an enormous tsunami. The waves swept across the ABZU within the southern part of the continent that we today are able to call Africa. The waves continued to move north over the whole land, rising into the valley that lies between the Tigris as well as the Euphrates rivers, which is where The great cities of the Anunnaki's had been built. The Anunnaki riding in their chariots of the sky were watching as the entire area was flooded by roaring waves. The flood of the oceans was followed by a massive torrent of rain that fell coming from the heavens. After forty days it was the time when the rains and thunderstorms were stopped and the floods started to receding.

While the Deluge occurred and the vessel carrying Ziusudra or Noah and his family sailed without incident through the water. The ship landed at the top of the mountain, which was known to Sumerians and the Akkadians Arrata. One of the first things that earthlings performed as they emerged from the vessel was build an altar to perform a ritual sacrifice, offering an ewe-lamb to express their gratitude to EN.KI to have spared their lives. The Anunnaki who were atop the earth from their chariots, could see the flames coming from the altar and walked towards it to discover the source of it.

EN.LIL was angry when he saw that a few earthlings had not suffered destruction. The king was angry at EN.KI for telling Earthlings of the impending flooding, however EN.KI replied that he had never violated his oath and not discuss the imminent catastrophe with earthlings. it was only the walls of the grass hut. Ziusudra might have heard the conversation. EN.LIL kept wailing but it was only when he realized that EN.KI declare that Ziusudra was his son. EN.LIL eventually relented, and his anger slowed down as did the water of the Deluge when he smelled the food being cooked and becoming extremely hungry..He recognized the need for mankind, and he advised that the earthlings that been through the flood receive seeds along with the necessary tools to grow them, in order for the earth to return to its fertile state and capable of supporting the life of. In the end, the descendants of KA.IN have also survived and EN.LIL indeed was pleased that the human race was not eliminated as it became clear that Nibiru's passage through the Earth resulted in the fabric of its environment to be weakened. The Primitive Workers were going to require money to go to Nibiru's help.

The Deluge signified the conclusion of the time period known to Anunnaki as the Olden Times. Anunnaki in the form of Olden Times (which, as stated above, started by the reign of King AN on Nibiru)..All information about the world was carved into stone for future generations to follow.. The Anunnaki know this area in the form of Gobekli Tepe. Baalbek serves as an alternative base for Anunnaki.

11,000 BC - 1. New Stone Age begins at the conclusion in the Pleistocene Ice Age as per the experts. (See 7,000 to 5,000)

11,000 BC to the present 11,000 bc to present Cenozoic Era; Quaternary Period The Recent Epoch.

10,000 BC. 10,500 BC Deluge closes and the Anunnaki based upon EN.LIL's request, split the Earth into zones.

* The river valley that is drained through the Tigris and Euphrates rivers that is now occupied primarily by the nation of Iraq will be given to EN.LIL and his family. Ziusudra's children, Shem and Japheth will reside in the valley.

* The region that will become occupied in the future millenia by the state that is Saudi Arabia is given the title Tilmun (i.e. the Land Of The Missiles) and is given to NIN.HUR.SAG.

*

To the west of The valley of Nile river, expanding southwards across the continent that is later to be named of Africa,

EN.KI along with his son MAR.DUK and his descendants assume charge. Ziusudra's son Ham is a resident there.

10,500 BC. The first time a shar was held following the Deluge The Anunnaki establish a new "Place of the Chariots in the midst of a new location was destroyed by floodwaters.

The site is set to be in the areas that are which are being drained by Nile river and several centuries later will come to be called Egypt. The land being flat and have no natural features can be utilized to land The Anunnaki form two "peaks" through the construction of four-sided pyramid-shaped constructions. The structures were designed by NINGISHZIDDA. The larger of both structures has been known as Ekur (i.e. House Which Like A Mountain Is).

In the Ekur there are galleries and chambers where crystals from Nibiru are kept. These crystals will then be employed to be used in a way to signal any spacecraft that is about to enter. In between the two pyramids a monument dedicated to the architect NINGISHZIDDA was built. Because the structure was built in the Age of the Lion according to the Nephilim custom, the monument is constructed to resemble the animal, only by incorporating his head. NINGISHZIDDA himself.

The control center for space ports platform is located on the top of Mount Moriah(the futuristic Jerusalem)

10,000 BC The Domestic Age begins in the in the region of

Mesopotamia. One of the first mammals to become domesticated (circa 9500 B.C.) was the dog, most likely for food. It is believed that the global population to have risen to 5 million by this point.

9,780 BC MARDUK Enki's son, the first born has the surname of RA and splits the throne over Egypt between his two sons ASAR (known as in Egyptian custom in the Egyptian tradition as Osiris) as well as SATU (known by the Egyptian traditions in the Egyptian tradition as Seth).

ASAR was his wife, ASTA and SATU espoused NEBAT and NEBAT, daughters of SHAMGAZ as the leader of the Igigi (i.e. the Nephilim who were making their home in the station in Lahmu/Mars with purposes of transporting silver to Earth towards Nibiru). ASAR and ASTA built their homes alongside his father MAR.DUK within the valley of the Nile river. Meanwhile, SATU and NEBAT built their homes with her father SHAMGAZ in the valley between the Tigris and Euphrates rivers.

NEBAT was in awe of her sister's home in the fertile valley of Nile and snatched at by her father. She questioned her husband every day about what the reasons they were not chosen to inherit these fertile lands. Her constant pestering led SATU to plot to kill his brother to take ASAR's land.

9.330 BC 9330 BC SATU 9.330 BC SATU Seth invites ASAR or Osiris to a dinner party where he gives his brother poisoned drinks at which point, after ASAR is gone and he has been laid in the coffin. The coffin is then sealed and then thrown into the sea.

ASAR was killed prior to when MAR.DUK as well as ASTA found the tombstone. MAR.DUK in spite of his sorrow had to accept the truth that his younger son SATU will inherit from the family planned for his eldest one, ASAR. MAR.DUK would have it made disclosed to ASTA that she was going to have the son of SATU in order to carry on the family lineage in a proper manner, but ASTA did not agree. The woman obtained sperm from the remains of her husband and impregnated her with the semen. The son of ASTA, HORON (known in the Egyptian culture in the Egyptian tradition as Horus) was born ASTA.

9,000 BC - the city of Jericho has been established, its ruins being radiocarbon and dated at around 9000 B.C. Jericho was identified as a city because of its defensive wall. It is evident that people from the city worked to safeguard their dwellings and the community. The city covers ten acres of land inside the massive walls of stone.

9000 to 7500 B.C. Mankind begins a new phase of civilisation referred to by The Pre-Pottery Neolithic, a period that saw the use of stone tools is changing to high-quality stone tools that have specific functions. Man continues to cultivate various species of animals and plants during the time. A form of wheat referred to as an einkorn, is grown out of its native habitat, in the region currently occupied by the nation of Syria. It is a plant that tends to thrive naturallly in Taurus as well as the Zagros mountains, was discovered at Tell Abu Hureyra and

Mureybat along the banks of the Euphrates river. This is evidence that people living in the region deliberately planted this plant.

9,000 years ago Evidence shows that there were people living on the Western continents part of the hemisphere. The question of whether they came to Asia through the Bering Strait landbridge has been speculated by numerous experts.

8.970 BC The "First Pyramid War' is fought. HORON Horus Horus who has grown to adulthood, sets off for Tilmun in The Land Of The Missiles, along with a band of faithful earthlings. They have weapons constructed of iron, which is a brand new metal, the secret for its making HORON is taught by his great-uncle GIBIL the son of EN.KI. Horons challenges SATU or Seth to a fight for revenge over his father's death, ASAR / Osiris. SATU insists that the contest only involves two of them and then demands HORON to a duel.

They fight during the night during the battle which ensues, SATU strikes HORON with the poisoned dart that causes the latter to sink to earth like he's in death. ASTA as she watches her son's death and cries out to NINGISHZIDDA for assistance. NINGISHZIDDA is on the scene and turns the poison that HORON's body has into blood that is benevolent which revives ASTA's son. Then, HORON goes after SATU as well, and they again get involved by a scuffle within their plane. The victorious HORON shoots SATU down. In bonds and blind in bonds, he's taken by HORON to a meeting of the Anunnaki which pronounces the verdict to allow him to live, even though not heirless and blind.

8,670 bc. The 'Second Pyramid War' occurs. DU.MUZI is the younger son of EN.KI finds affection with INANNA NAN.NAR's daughter. NAN.NAR and grandchild of EN.LIL. However, their union is not without risk and the events that follow will lead the ancestors of EN.LIL into conflict with those of EN.KI.

EN.KI provided DU.MUZI and INANNA an extensive region to the north of the Abzu where they could live and govern after their wedding. MAR.DUK, DU.MUZI's older brother was unhappy with DU.MUZI. When INANNA informed GESHTINANNA DU.MUZI along with MAR.DUK's sister about their dream of creating a huge kingdom, GESHTINANNA visited MAR.DUK and explained everything to him.

MAR.DUK came up with a scheme to defraud DU.MUZI as well as INANNA of the legal heir. MAR.DUK got GESHTINANNA to DU.MUZI for the purpose of being immunized by him. In Anunnaki traditions, a children born to a brother and sister had more legitimacy with respect to inheritance over one who was born to siblings who were not.

After he had sex with his sister GESHTINANNA, DU.MUZI dreamt that the punishment was severe and that he had his kingdom was taken from the man. The dreamer awoke, and informed his wife GESHTINANNA what he had dreamed about. Although he was extremely disoriented by the dream GESHTINANNA put the idea to him that maybe it was a signification of the moment MAR.DUK discovered they were in bed with each other, he'd think that DU.MUZI was raped by his sister. DU.MUZI believed that the suggestion of GESHTINANNA was true as he ran away from her. In the course of his escape, DU.MUZI came upon a stream, and after slipping over his feet on the rock, he became drowned by the river.

INANNA her lover, DU.MUZI She was stricken grieving. In the news, it was revealed by INANNA that DU.MUZI's dead body was floating within the waters of the river up to Abzu which was where her sister,

ERESH.KIGAL, reigned. Thus to Abzu she went to recover the body of her love. ERESH.KIGAL believed INANNA of plotting something that wasn't true; she believed that the stricken lover was trying to obtain an heir through their husband NER.GAL who then put her in chains to the stake.

Discovering what happened among ERESH.KIGAL AND INANNA, EN.KI fashioned two "emissaries" from clay sending them to the Abzu in order to secure the release of and the return of INANNA. They discovered INANNA however, her vital spirit had departed her body. The members of the emissaries sprinkled Water Of Life upon her and resurrected her. They went back to the "upper world' along with INANNA as well as the corpse of DU.MUZI.

INANNA requested that EN.KI must punish MAR.DUK because of his involvement in the demise of DU.MUZI. EN.KI responded that, although MAR.DUK could have been responsible for the incidents that drove

DU.MUZI to his final death, he cannot be considered to be responsible for his murder. INANNA was then able to contact her parents to plead to them for revenge against MAR.DUK.

EN.LIL delivered a letter to EN.KI asking for MAR.DUK's surrender to INANNA's family INANNA and INANNA, which EN.KI did not agree. The second Second Pyramid War erupted between the families of EN.LIL and EN.KI.

Spacecrafts armed with nuclear weapons The two families battled against each other. In the land that were inhabited by the Annunnaki the destruction was extensive as well as hundreds of innocent Anunnaki as well as earthlings were murdered. Then, pursued by INANNA, MAR.DUK hid himself inside the Ekur, the only great structure that was designed by his brother NINGISHZIDDA. EN.LIL's Son, NIN.URTA found the secret access into the Ekur which he then as well as INANNA as well as ISH.KUR were able to pursue MAR.DUK through the pathways. In the chamber above the Ekur MAR.DUK dropped the stone locks that slide to ensure that the fugitives could not pursue him further. While in the chamber EN.LIL's children ripped open the ropes holding the stones that were blocking him. They moved into the chamber, securing MAR.DUK in the chamber.

SARPANIT who was the wife of MAR.DUK visited EN.KI and asked him to release the husband's freedom. EN.KI told her to meet with NAN.NAR as well as his kids, UTU and INANNA to appeal to save MAR.DUK's life. However, INANNA refused to give up.

EN.KI and EN.LIL requested NIN.HUR.SAG to be mediator. She ruled that, even though MAR.DUK was to be punished but he was not deserving to be killed. It was therefore agreed that MAR.DUK could be released from the grave of his imprisonment, however the he had to move to an area where none of the earthlings resided.

NINGISHZIDDA and her husband, NINGISHZIDDA, who built the famous Ekur was summoned to discover a method to free MAR.DUK from the bowels of his.

In the wake of being told about the terms of his release MAR.DUK began to rage. In the end the man accepted his fate as he, his wife, and their son NABU went to those lands that were inhabited by Anunnaki and earthlings.

This was the time that the Great Pyramid was destroyed by Ninurta and invading forces also removed the crystals and some melted away, so it could not be used again.

EN.KI, EN.LIL and NIN.HUR.SAG connected to their father ANU who had visited them. GALZU was making many times prior to the visit, in order to relay to the Anunnaki and their descendants the Nephilim "who came down were from Heaven fell, and ANU's warning to not go back to Nibiru so that they would not be killed by the effects

Earth's orbital size had caused to their bodies. It was a shock to ANU He had never had an emissary or a representative, or known about GALZU. He even told his children that there existed solutions that would heal the body ravages due to the changes that planetary cycle had brought about.

ANU confessed to his children that it became clear to him that it was in the Will of God the Creator of all that Earthlings, and not the Anunnaki would be the ones to be the inheritors of the Earth. Thus, ANU declared, it was the duty of the Anunnaki to ensure that kingship was established in the Earth that would be given to an chosen Earthling as well as to educate the Earthlings the basics of the sciences and religion.

At first it is believed that the Earth could be split into four areas in which Earthlings' unique kind of society could, with the help of the Anunnaki develop and flourish.

*The First Region was to encompass those lands that the Edin was in existence prior to it was absorbed by the Deluge (i.e. the valley that was formed by the Tigris and Euphrates Rivers - later known as Shumer as well as Mesopotamia). EN.LIL along with his children were selected to oversee the Earthlings in the area. It was the First Region was also known under the title of Ki-Engi (i.e. "the Land of the Lofty Watchers).

* The second Region included The Land of the Two Narrows (i.e. The Nile Valley - later known as Egypt or Nubia). EN.KI along with his children were tasked with shepherding the Earthlings in the valley.

*The Third Region was intended to include all the areas located to the east of First Region (i.e. in the Indus Valley). INANNA was to lead the Earthlings to the Indus Valley.

*The Fourth Region would encompass all the areas that lie on the peninsula referred to by the name of Place of the Chariots (i.e. the region that would eventually get the designation of Sinai Peninsula). Sinai Peninsula). The Fourth Region was to be reserved to the Anunnaki.

Anu examines all regions and travels on across South America where Ninurta had created a house to him using a exquisitely cut stones, encased in gold.

ANU as well as his wife, ANTU, as part of their trip on their trip to South America, traveled to the land where MARDUK was exiled. Then they discovered EN.KI's son EN.KI living in a solitary home along with his son NABU as well as his spouse and SARPANIT had lost her life. ANU felt sorry for MAR.DUK and declared that he would be relieved from his exile. Despite being rebuked of ANU, MAR.DUK was angered over the notion that INANNA would be charged with the responsibility of a particular region.

The Enlilship (i.e. the kingship) in the land that were part of the Nile valley was handed over to NIN.URTA. In this time when Heliopolis was established as a city. Heliopolis was founded as a beacon city.'

7500 BC - A cemetery first appears on the continent of North in the Western hemisphere.

75,000 to 5,000 B.C. The time period of the Neolithic is superior to the Paleolithic. The Neolithic is also referred to as the "New Stone Age' (sometimes noted as encompassing the Pre-Pottery Neolithic period from 9,000 to 7,500 B.C.) It is the time where primitive stone tools were replaced with high-quality stone tools that have particular roles. The rapid growth of pottery, which became in the early 7000 B.C., emphasizes the cultivation of grain like barley and wheat, to usage as a primary supply of foodstuffs. Certain types of metals, including gold and copper, began to become discovered and refined in regions of modern-day Europe and in the Near East.

7700 to 6,000 BC - Sheep was domesticated from as early as 9,500 within the Zagros mountains of Mesopotamia However, to the southwest of the Levantine region, which is encompassed by the current nations comprising Syria, Jordan and Lebanon The animal that was introduced to the domestic market is gazelle. This follows by the goat around the age of 7,000 B.C. The domestication of pigs is occurring currently in the area that is encompassed in the current time by Turkey. Cattle were domesticated within the Aegean area by the year the year 6,000 B.C.

6500 BC - 6,500 bc. Bronze Age begins in the area of Mesopotamia.

Between 6,500 and 5,500 BC The introduction of agriculture to the area that is encompassing the modern-day nations from Greece as well as Bulgaria. The first communities appear on the Danube River by 5,500 B.C.

6,250 to 5,400 BC Catal Huyuk is the largest city in the area commonly called Anatolia that will later be known as the name that refer to Asia Minor and Turkey. The city covers an area of around 32 acres.

In the year 6,000 BC, rice is the main crop throughout Asia and in the area of modern-day Thailand.

5500 BC Cotton is grown throughout the Indus Valley. Over the next ten years, a closely related variety of the plant will grow in the Western northern hemisphere.

Between 5,300 and 4,750 BC Communities of farmers are seen within the current region of France.

5,300-5,000 BC Cities can be seen all over in the Mesopotamian alluvial plain that is fed via the Tigris and Euphrates rivers. Around the same time that it is at this time that the Nile Valley is colonized.

From 5,000 to 2,500 B.C. The region is populated by farming communities. zone now covered by China. By 2,500 B.C. Walled cities and states appear. The production of precious gems including jade starts.

4500 BC. Agriculture expands across the area now occupied by Germany and northern Europe.

4,004 BC - Traditional Hebrew date of the Creation that lasted over seven days.

The plough first appears around this point in Sumer.

4,400 BC. The cultivation of rice expands into in the Yangtze delta region in modern-day China.

4000 The spread of agriculture extends across the islands that are now part of Ireland and the British Isles and Ireland.

4000 to 3000 bc It is the time when there's a onset of desiccation across the northern part of the African continent, creating the desert later to be known as the Sahara. In this time inhabitants of this region are compelled to move eastwards to the area drained by Nile River, or southward towards the area that is drained by Congo River.

3,800 BC The oldest evidence of civilization found in Sumer that dates back up to 3,800 B.C., is uncovered on an area called Eridu during the 1920s in the early years.

3,800 bc ~ The Anunnaki re-establish the 'Olden Cities' of Eridu and Nibru-Ki (aka Nippur). In the middle of this period, ANU comes to Earth again. ANU observes that the more pronounced rotation of the Earth within the solar system and the shorter time between night and day are causing his children to get older faster as the other Nibiruans.

It is believed that the city Unug-Ki (i.e. Uruk in Akkadian also known as Erech from the Hebrew Bible) was built to honor the ANU.

After ANU's trip to Earth in the year 2000, the Anunnaki declared that, from then on the time span must be measured, not by shars like the case with Nibiru however, it should be measured in Earth orbital years. The idea of a calendar was formulated which first came into existence on Nippur.

3,760 B.C. Traditional Hebrew date of the first appearance of Adam and Eve.

3,760 BC Kingship transfers to Earthlings in Kishi. The time-keeping process in Earth years has started.

The Anunnaki started to teach Earthlings sciences in mathematics, religion and math according to what ANU was directing. The Earthlings conferred the title of Lofty Lords to the Anunnaki and their habitations of the Lofty Lords were granted the name temples.

City of Kishi was the first city to be specifically designed for Earthlings. The city's name Kishi was a reference to the Scepter City. There was a place where NIN.URTA along with the ME of kingship that came from EN.KI awarded kingship to the Earthlings and was appointed as the first human king.

Incredulous about NIN.URTA's ability to guide his fellow Earthlings in the First Region in their path towards kingship INANNA planned to extort the Me's of civilization as well as the title of king from EN.KI in order to bestow the title of king upon the Earthlings from the Third Region, whom she was given the task of overseeing. Then she went to EN.KI's residence, and after after consuming him in a rogue way, she stole the ninety-four ME's necessary for the establishment of civilization and kingship. After he uncovered the incident, EN.KI called on EN.LIL to request to return the ME's to his daughter.

INANNA said she was claiming that EN.KI has voluntarily given her ME's as well as it was EN.LIL's conclusion that her claim was legitimate. The king ordered that, when the reign of kingship in Kishi is over and the right to kingship would pass to Unug-Ki. Although this pleased INANNA it angered MAR.DUK since the kingship ought to have been properly moved to his First Region to the Second Region in which EN.KI along with his brothers had the responsibility of guiding the Earthlings.

MAR.DUK and his son NABU called the Igigi together with their Earthling descendants from across the globe on the earth to make their way to Edin to assist in creating a holy city where MAR.DUK was to reign. The city was named by him Bab-Ili (i.e. Babylon, the Gateway of the Gods). The followers of his were engaged in building an elevated tower that could'reach the skies in the sky' or have the ability to speak directly with Nibiru.

EN.LIL attempted to stop MAR.DUK as he created the Earthlings in their language to become disorientated, and they wouldn't be able to comprehend each other. The incident occurred during the 310th year after the accounting for Earth year had started (i.e. 3,450).

Between 2,500 and 3,500 B.C. 3,500 to 2,500 bc. Sumerian city-states thrive. There are around twelve cities located in the Mesopotamian Plain that make up Sumer. The culture also thrived during the time of Sumer (i.e. Shinar, Shumer). The extensive use of ploughs here can be a sign of agricultural society. The evolution of the wheel shows the wisdom of the people and their mastery in the mathematics from the Sumerians. Cities are fed with a canal system and dams that show an impressive amount of planning and co-ordination between the different cities.

Sippar was the city that Sippar was rebuilt by UTU Then, from Sippar, he was able to impart wisdom about justice to Earthlings.

Adab was the city that Adab was created in order to accommodate NIN.HUR.SAG to serve as a place of healing as well as the dissemination of medical wisdom. The temple where NIN.HUR.SAG lived became the home of ME's that related to the evolution of genes and alteration of the Earthlings.

Chapter 5: city in the state of Urim was founded by NAN.NAR

INANNA was a resident of The city of Unug-Ki.

3,372 BC Mayan calendar's initial date starts.

3,350 BC - Kingship transfer to Kishi to Sumer to Unug-Ki within the Third Region, the Indus Valley.

3,200 B.C. - The very first written inscriptions are discovered. These are accounts of merchants' evidence found in Tell Brak in northern Mesopotamia.

3200-2,000 BC 3200-2,000 BC Cycladic civilization thrives within the Aegean region.

3,110 BC 3,110 BC MAR.DUK with his son NINGISHZIDDA dispute over which among the two sons from EN.KI is the rightful representative to be the Lord of the Second Region. To make peace between them, EN.KI requests that NINGISHZIDDA be a slave to his elder brother and locate a new place the region where he can live. NINGISHZIDDA in obedience to the wishes that his dad has made, has left his home in the Nile Valley, and with an army of faithful fans, journeys across Earth in search of a new home in the regions of the continent that lies on the other end of the ocean. The new home of NINGISHZIDDA is also known as"the Winged Serpent. He creates a brand new system of method of accounting for time.

3100-3000 bc. Written writing in the form pictographs has been developed since Sumer. The usage of pictographs to communicate spreads across Mesopotamia eastwards to the area called in the early world by the name of Elam (i.e. Elam is the region that forms the boundary between the modern-day nations that are Iraq as well as Iran) in the southwest, and then toward Egypt. In the first 2,000 years B.C. The Sumerian pictographs were transformed into cuneiform. Elamite pictographs would evolve into a cuneiform form called Linear Elamite; and in Egypt the pictographs will develop into distinctive hieroglyphs for the country. Beginning with Elam it is believed that the usage of pictographs will expand further to the east, to the Indus Valley civilization as well as later to the Asian civilizations that are currently developing in China.

The Egyptian hieroglyphs will expanded all the way to Peloponnesian island in Crete which is expected to evolve by 1500 B.C., into a version of the hieroglyphic alphabet, that is the precursor of two writing styles known in the form of Linear A and Linear B script. The Egyptian hieroglyphs will spread to the east into Palestine and Palestine, from where it is expected to evolve into an alphabet known as the Canaanite alphabet. In the meantime, Sumerian cuneiform script will be spread across Asia Minor (i.e. Anatolia which is also known as today's

Turkey) and is expected to evolve into Hittite and Hurrian versions of the cuneiform. The Sumerian cuneiform may also expanded throughout Palestine and into the Levantine area (i.e. the present-day region of Syria, Lebanon and Jordan) in which case it would be merged into the Canaanite alphabet and become the Ugaritic alphabet sometime between 1500 and 1000 B.C.

3,100 B.C. - 3100 bc Menes connects the kingdoms of lower and upper of Egypt and establishes the notion of the "pharaoh" as god-king. His reign is the culmination of more than 350 years of war within the Nile valley. The reign of his father was the first dynasty of thirty-one to govern Egypt for the duration of 2 and two-and-a-half millennia.

Based on a connection with Egyptian practices and those from the past Sumer When MAR.DUK declared his claim to the title of shepherd in the Second Region, the

'Land of Two Narrows', as it was known, and the Nile Valley was known, He changed his name in to RA (i.e. The Bright One). The father of his son, EN.KI had been praised for his role as PTAH (i.e. the developer). The Anunnaki were first recognized as the Second Region by the name of the Neteru the Guardian Watchers.

RA or MARDUK united the two kingdoms that existed on the Nile during that time and became one kingdom. It also appointed MENA as an offspring of Neteru as well as an Earthling as the first king of the kingdom. The King Mena or Menes is a part of the descent from the Anunnaki or Neteru and with their blood running through his veins, he was able to take the title pharaoh meaning 'god-king.'

RA constructed for Menes a 'scepter city, so that it could surpass Kishi in terms of beauty. It was christened Mena-Nefer (i.e. Mena's Beauty).

To help his son's newly-formed area, EN.KI / PTAH gave to MARDUK and RA ME's to help him impart knowledge of civilization to Earthlings in the Second Region. Every ME other than the one that informed about the eternal existence was handed over to RA to benefit his son the civilisation that developed to maturity along the Nile Valley became very rich in understanding the sciences of religion and science.

3100 to 26855 bc In the Early Dynastic Period in Egypt huge advances are being made in the fields of construction of stones, copper smelting and other crafts of every kind.

3000 BC - 3000 bc Indus Valley civilization is flourishing with two major cities (Harappa Mohenjo-Daro and Harappa) along with nearly seventy small cities.

Part of the Third Region would become known as Zamash which is the Land of Sixty Precious Stones. A different part was referred to by the title of Aratta which is the Wooded Realm.

To INANNA EN.KI will not offer ANY ME'S OTHER THAN those that she'd already had through deceit, taken from him.

3,500 to 2,750 B.C. the Bronze Age flourishes in the area of Palestine.

INANNA was obsessed by the notion that her dear DU.MUZI might one day return from the grave to stay with her for eternity. In her mind, she created the Gigunu the House of Nighttime Pleasure, where she would draw young men during the evening of their weddings. Then she would lie with them and later when they woke up, their unlived corpses would be discovered.

One young man did not die after a night at Gigunu. He was BANDA and through his body blood from UTU was pumped. He became ENMERKAR as the king of Unug-Ki and also was married to NINSUN an ancestor of EN.LIL. to BANDA the couple

NINSUN had a child named GILGAMESH. The son of BANDA questioned his mother on the demise of Earthlings and also the immortality of gods, called the Nephilim who from which he was a descendant. NINSUN said to GILGAMESH that for as any Earthling or Anunnaki lived on the Earth and died, they'd die in a death sentence, however people who resided in Nibiru would live longevity. Therefore, GILGAMESH desired to travel to Nibiru.

NINSUN made an appeal to UTU to aid her son's journey to Nibiru. UTU ultimately agreed to help, but GILGAMESH had to undertake his way towards Nibiru to the Landing Place of the Chariots in the fourth Region(Baalbek) by himself. UTU was aware that EN.LIL has created a fire-belching monster that was able to protect the Landing Place, and that should GILGAMESH was determined and courageous enough to conquer this challenge then he'd be able go towards Nibiru. 2,760 BC. However, the civilisation in the Third Region does not blossom like it could. The shepherd who is there, INANNA, covets the Second Region and that is part of the Nile Valley, and she ignores her own. 11,000 Earth years later, after the counting of time started, reign of the king is taken away by Unug-Ki. In the past the hero Gilgamesh is set off on an grand adventure to live a longevity. GILGAMESH defeated the beast which sat in the Landing Place, and made his way through the fourth Region's tunnels that are subterranean. Through his explorations, GILGAMESH came upon ZIUSUDRA as well as his wife, EMZARA, who related the story of the Deluge and informed the boy hero of the plant that grew in a water source that taking of would give them a longer lifespan. It was his travels to Nibiru not being necessary, should there was a chance to get the plant that gave them longevity here in the world of Earth, GILGAMESH by stealth took the plant out of the well and raced back to Unug Ki.

When he returned towards Unug-Ki, GILGAMESH became tired and tired and sleepy. While he slept the snake was drawn to the smell of the plant GILGAMESH kept inside his bag. It snuck through the satchel of GILGAMESH and then ate the plant before vanishing. GILGAMESH was awake and realized the situation, but the only thing he could do was to return empty-handed and angry in Unug-Ki.

Following GILGAMESH There was seven more kings who were in charge of the Third Region, but then just one millennium after gaining kingship the kingship was lost.

2,760 BC The reign of kingship passes from the Unug-Ki region to Urim under the guidance that of NAN.NAR along with NIN.GAL. The cities in the First Region, of Sumer thrive under their direction as civilization expands into the adjacent regions. The reign of the king is not centered by any single city, it is rotated throughout the entire region.

2686-2160 B.C. The empire referred to as the "Old Kingdom" (i.e. the time of Pyramid construction) starts in Egypt. Imhotep constructs his first Pyramid, which was a one-way structure that was built to honor his king Zoser who was a king at Saqqara.

MARDUK/RA, in awe of the rise of civilization and culture in Sumer and beware of allowing another Anunnaki or Earthling to take over his reign then declared that he alone would serve as the ruler of the Second Region.

MARDUK / RA also undertook the process of rewriting history. MARDUK or RA declared that priests who prayed for him as well as the Earthlings in the Nile Valley should proclaim that he, RA was the 'eldest from Heaven and firstborn living on Earth. MARDUK / RA also decreed that priests would be singing hymns to him because he was they were the first from the very beginning of time' as well as being the Lord of Eternity, the one who has everlasting power his mark over the gods in the throne', and as "one without comparison and is the most singular and only one and the only one!' MARDUK / RA then took on the characteristics and power that were the attributes and powers of different gods (i.e. the Anunnaki who were the Earthlings were referred to as gods').

MAR.DUK said / RA had a determination to lead the whole Earth in the name of his father EN.KI.

2500 BC - In attempts to control over Gold mining as well as trade of the Kush within the Nubian Desert In order to control the Nubian Desert, the Egyptians take on their neighbor to the south and take over the area to the south of it was the Second Cataract of the Nile.

2,500 years ago - The horse was domesticated in Asia.

2,380 bc. Amorites of Arabia begin to conquer and conquer regions like Syria, Palestine and Mesopotamia.

2371 - 2,316 B.C. 2,371 to 2,316 bc Sumerian city-states have been united into Akkadia beneath the Semitic Amorite ruler, Sharru-Kin (i.e. Sargon the Great). The city of capitalization is located in the vicinity of Kishi and named Agade (i.e. Akkad). Akkad. Akkadian Empire, the world's first great empire in time, spans all the way from to the Zagros Mountains in the east and extends to the Mediterranean Sea in the west.

To counter MAR.DUK's plans for global dominance, EN.LIL and his children wanted to create an Earthling ruler to defend their rights. They selected Sharru-Kin (i.e. The Righteous Regent) who was who was the son of Arbakad.

2,350 BC Merchants' first appearance occurs in temple accounts of Lagash. Later, trading areas occur in all cities across Mesopotamia.

2,316 bc. SharruKin took part of the holy soil from Babylon in the area where MAR.DUK was attempting to construct a tower that would reach the sky. The soil was removed, and put in Agade where it was erected the 'Heavenly Bright Obscure.'

MAR.DUK was informed of the Sharru-Kin's decision to remove the sacred soil, became angry by jealousy. He thought that only he should be the one to own the sacred soil that a "gateway to gods' might be built. Thus to his home in the First Region MAR.DUK traveled, along with his son NABU along with others, began the building of a new Babili that is known as the Gateway of the Gods, at the same site as the one he had made a thousand times before.

MAR.DUK's actions created chaos. INANNA took on MAR.DUK's new settlement, which murdered some of his supporters during the attack. The destruction and loss of lives is said to be the most devastating ever recorded by the Earthlings. NER.GAL requested his brother MAR.DUK for him to leave Mesopotamia, the First Region, of which there was no legitimate heir, so that bloodshed wouldn't continue. MAR.DUK finally relented, and he quit the area of Mesopotamia.

2,305 BC 2,305 BC Terah is the father of Nahor is birthed at Ur in the Chaldees. Terah is eventually his father. Abram (i.e. Abraham Abu-Ramu), Nahor and Haran and from them will descend people like those of the Israelites, Ishmaelites, Midianites, Moabites and the Ammonites. Terah died around 2,100 B.C. and at an age of 205.

Also known as Tirhu as per the Sumerian text, Terah was chosen by EN.LIL in order to be the source of seed to create a vast country of Earthlings. EN.LIL was visited by the prophet GALZU and was advised that there was going to begin a time of immense bloodshed and ill-will that was brought on by MAR.DUK. EN.LIL was warned that in three celestial sections that the Ram of MAR.DUK was to take over EN.LIL's personal. GALZU cautioned EN.LIL to be alert that MAR.DUK has previously declared that he was supreme Anunnaki god, could unleash war and destruction in order to prove that assertion. EN.LIL was told to select one of the Earthling like Ziusudra or Noah was previously chosen to serve the goal of conserving the seeds that was the Earthlings.

Tirhu or Terah is an oracle-priest and an ancestor of Arbakad as well as six generations of Nibru-Ki priests.

EN.LIL directed NAN.NAR, his son NAN.NAR to construct an urban area in between Tigris and Euphrates rivers which would be named Haran and in which Tirhu or Terah was to be declared the priest-prince.

2,291 years ago Naram Sin, the grandchild of Sharru-Kin is elevated to the throne of Akkad.

In the time of Naram-Sin's, INANNA was able to seize an opportunity to pursue her personal ambition. Discovering that EN.LIL as well as NIN.URTA were leaving their home in the First Region to travel to the territories that lay across the oceans and discovering that MAR.DUK was a momentarily departed from to the Second Region, INANNA felt it was time for her to stake claim to the areas.

INANNA revealed her authority to Naram-Sin. She commanded Naram-Sin to raise an army of her in her honor to conquer the kingdoms of Magan and Meluhha within the Nile Valley. Naturally, to accomplish this, Naram-Sin was required to traverse his way across the Sinai Peninsula, the sacred Fourth Region.

2260 BC - Naram-Sin succeeded in his war however, news about his work was reported to EN.LIL angry He returned to the territories that comprised the 4 regions. EN.LIL cursed Naram-Sin as well as the Akkadian kingdom he controlled. Through this curse, Naram Sin was soon killed through the bite of scorpions, and the Akkadian empire Akkad became unstable.

The kingship was transferred from city to city including those of Earthlings and the Anunnaki. In the end, EN.LIL was in consultation together with his father ANU and the two determined that NAN.NAR was to be the position of shepherd in the First Region of Mesopotamia.

2,200 years ago - Bronze Age in Ireland begins.

2,180 BC 2.180 BC - At the close of VIth Dynasty, the Old Kingdom of Egypt was dissolved.

Between 2,180 and 2,040 BC 2,040 to 2,180 bc First Intermediate Period of Egypt starts with the fall of the Old Kingdom. While there were kings situated at Memphis and then at Heracleopolis The actual authority is derived from provincial governors as well as"nomarchs" who form their own army and collect taxes to fund their own 'nomes.'

2,180 BC 2180 BC MARDUK 2,180 BC MARDUK RA remains in power in the Upper Kingdom (i.e. southern Egypt) in contrast to Pharaohs who oppose him have supremacy within the Lower Kingdom (i.e. the northern region of Egypt).

2,170 BC the Dragon Court in the Ankhfn-khonsu was established in Egypt.

2,161 bc ~ Abram (i.e. Abraham Ibru-Um, Abu Ramu, etc.) was born in Ur "of the Chaldees. In accordance with Hebrew traditions, Abram descends from Shem the child of Noah which is the ninth generation of Shem.

Between 2,113 and 2,006 B.C. 2,113 to 2,006 bc. Akkadian empire collapses as the Sumerians recapture the control. About 2006 in 2006, around 2006, Elamites from Persia as well as Amorites from Arabia and Amorites from Arabia take over and conquer Sumer.

2,113 BC The reign in the First Region was granted to Ur, the city of Urim (i.e. Ur) and Ur-Nammu was named king.

2100 BC - The Amorites discovered Babylon. Babylon.

2,096 BC Ur-Nammu dies mortally wounded in combat. The Earthlings regard his tragic death as an act of betrayal to EN.LIL as well as the Anunnaki and the Anunnaki, who have become increasingly removed from the human world.

2,095 BC Shulgi takes the throne of Ur following the demise of Ur-Nammu. During Shulgi's rule his reign, the Sumerian kingdom prospers. Shulgi is regarded for being a man who is fervent to fight; and to that his end, he enlists warriors of the mountains (i.e. Elamites) that aren't subordinate to NAN.NAR. Under his rule, Shulgi became the lover of INANNA.

2,090 B.C. As per Hebrew custom, around seventy-years old, Abram is called by God and his god, Jehovah and is commanded to leave Ur and move towards "a land that I will show thee." The first destination is Haran located north of Ur and alongside Nahor's family.

According to Hebrew traditions, after the passing of his father Terah, Abram was again received by God He told him to go over the Euphrates River and then travel southward to Canaan (i.e. the southern region of Syria that borders on the Mediterranean Sea). The time came when Abram was directed by God to depart from his family members, which is why together with his wife Sarah as well as his nephew, Lot, he began his journey to the south. In establishing an encampment in the Valley of Moreh, God again approached Abram and offered him an assurance that his seed (i.e. his descendants) will one day own the land.

The Hebrew story does not define the reasons God gave the blessing to Abram as well as the specifics of what Abram had to do or was already doing, to receive the promise isn't mentioned within the Hebrew Bible. The Sumerian text, on the contrary, reveal that EN.LIL addressed Ibru-Um the son of Tirhu to instruct him to journey to Canaan for the purpose of protecting the sacred places at the Place of the Celestial Chariots in the Sinai Peninsula, in order to ensure that the Anunnaki Chariots would continue to fly safely and landings.

Abram, Sarah and Lot continued to travel further south towards Egypt and, in the fear that the Pharaoh may want to acquire his wife for his own, Abram instructed Sarah to be his sister and to not receive any punishment by the Pharoah.

According to the Unger's Bible Dictionary (by Merrill F. Unger The year is 1957.) sister is another term for niece, the connection to that Sarah was actually had to Abram. According to Zecharia Sitchin's book Genesis Revisited, Sarah was actually the "sister" of Abram and, despite having the identical mother, their parents differed. The older Sumerian and Akkadian sources have proven that the norm of the Nephilim and Anunnaki was the practice of a man to be mated with his half-sister via that same parent. It is believed that the practice was learned by this custom was handed down to the Sumerians as well, who also followed this practice.

Like he had expected, Sarah was claimed by the Pharaoh and returned to his house to be kept as a concubine. In exchange for her, the Pharaoh offered Abram numerous valuable possessions. After the Pharaoh was aware of the ruse and reclaimed the concubine, he handed over Sarah to Abram and then ordered the trio to go home; however, the Pharaoh did not insist that the riches of gifts be taken away, even though. So, Abram, Sarah and Lot returned to the country of Canaan.

The wealth that Abram had just acquired Abram turned into a cause that caused a lot of disagreement between Abram and his nephew Lot. It was not apparent adequate to feed the flocks of Abram as well as Lot and so Abram offered Lot the option of choosing the property. Lot picked the plain of Jordan while leaving the areas in the vicinity of Hebron to Abram. Because of his selflessness, God came to Abram and blessed his faith with a promise to create numerous descendants.

2,076 BC after their return at Canaan, Abram and Sarah (now aged 75 years) did not have children. Sarah convinced Abram to marry her Egyptian handmaiden Hagar with whom she bore Abram one son. He was called Ishmael.

2,062 bc. As Abram was ninety-nine years old in age, God returned to his face and changed his surname to Abraham. God kept the promise He was previously making with Abram by reassuring Abraham that the descendants of his son would be diverse.

2,061 bc. The son, called Isaac was the son of Abraham who was then 100 years old as well as his wife Sarah who was then ninety years old.

2,036 BC 236 BC God obliges Abraham to trial, asking him to undertake the sacrifice of his first born son Isaac aged 25 years old. Abraham was diligently tackling the job to prepare for the sacrifice at Mount Moriah. The king was about sink in the son's heart who he placed in the altar of sacrifice however his hand was secured by the angels from the Lord. In addition, because he was open to accepting the commands from God even in the case of his son to the Lord, the Lord reiterated the agreement He previously had established.

Abrahamic Covenant Abrahamic Covenant, which God made Abraham Abram Abraham Abraham was comprised of six components:

* "I will make of thee a great nation"

* "I will bless thee"

* "And make thy name great"

* "And thou shalt be a blessing"

* "I will bless them that bless thee and curse him that curseth thee"

* "In thee shall all the families of the earth be blessed"

2,060 to 1,785 BC 2.060-1,785 B.C. Middle Kingdom of Egypt is caused by

through the rulers by the monarchs Thebes through the subjugation of the nomes to the south of Thebes followed through a sweep northwards towards Heracleopolis. This triumph is achieved by Mentuhotep II who gets rid of foreign (i.e. Asiatic as well as

Libyan) colonists from the Delta region of the Nile. In the Middle Kingdom will be noted as a pioneer in the development of arts and the culture. (Note that some scholars place to the Middle Kingdom between the years between 2,040 and 1,750 B.C.)

2,055 bc Shulgi may be acting under the instructions of NAN.NAR who is given the task of repressing the unrest that has erupted in Canaan by enlisting the aid of his Elamite combatants. However, he doesn't stay at the frontier of Canaan as well as Sinai. In complete disregard for the sacred redness and beauty of that Fourth Region on the Sinai Peninsula, Shulgi overruns it and proclaims himself to be the The King of the Four Regions.

2,048 B.C. - As per the Sumerian sources, it was the time when EN.LIL requested Ibru-Um at the time living with his family in Haran and Haran, to travel to the south in order to protect the holy Place of the Celestial Chariots.

2,047 bc ~ After Shulgi's death, Amar-Sin (i.e. Amraphel) takes over as the king of Ur.

2,041 BC Amar-Sin together with others kings of the First Region, under the supervision of INANNA starts a war to take over the Fourth Region. However, he fails it only increases the support of MARDUK and his plan to form an army the area of Haran shortly after Ibru-Um / Abram had left the region.

MAR.DUK declared that the age of the ram was the time for him to reign and he informs his fellow Anunnaki that this was his goal, after suffering enough in their hands due to the wrongs he truly committed however, in return for the same sins he payed and was now planning return to into the First Region and establish a temple there. From which he would be able to reign. MAR.DUK announces that the age of the Ram was in hand.Ningishzidda creates stone observatories in order in order to demonstrate this.

Along with his followers, MAR.DUK made his way south towards Sumer and built his temple in Babylon. His followers' army wreaked destruction throughout Mesopotamia and also ruined Nippur, the Holy of Holies at Nippur. There was a revelation that his main plan to capture and retain control over the spaceport referred to for its location as the Place of the Celestial Chariots within the Fourth Region on the Sinai Peninsula.

The remaining Anunnaki attended a meeting in the council, and everyone, even MAR.DUK's brothers himself accepted that MARDUK's desire to be the ultimate god among them needed to be thwarted once and all. The only exception was EN.KI expressed a disapproving opinion. The ENKI group believed that the remaining Anunnaki must accept the path of destiny that foretold the supremacy of MARDUK. They will not be influenced by the plan of their leaders to end MARDUK.

The Anunnaki were of the opinion that the best option was to eliminate Nibiru's Place of the Celestial Chariots with nuclear weapons, which they identified as Weapons of Terror. In the event of Nibiru's Place of the Celestial Chariots destroyed, all travel routes towards and back from Nibiru will be shut off for all. However, it is worthwhile to make sure that MARDUK could not restrict travel to or from Nibiru and his concept of supremacy would be ineffective.

The Anunnaki council agreed Anunnaki who were in council with MARDUK to NIN.URTA and NER.GAL who are brothers of EN.LIL and ENKI, must take over the devastation of the Place of the Celestial Chariots.

2,024 BC Weapons of Terror are used for first time on globe Earth. It is the Place of the Celestial Chariots is destroyed by nuclear weapons, and the Evil Wind destroys the Sumerian civilisation.

Through the aid of ABGAL, EN.KI had concealed his Weapons of Terror numerous shars in the past, before EN.LIL's entry into the Earth in order to stop ALALU from being able to locate and use these weapons. EN.KI believed that nobody except him knew where they was. Unbeknownstto EN.KI, EN.LIL had discovered the hidden location of these Weapons of Terror.

EN.LIL was able to inform NIN.URTA as well as NER.GAL of the mountain where they discovered the Weapons of Terror had been hiding, and then gave them instructions on how to equip them in order to fire.

EN.LIL advised NIN.URTA as well as NER.GAL to ensure that they did not to injure any one of the Anunnaki that might be present at their destination at the Place of the Celestial Chariots as well as to provide them with an opportunity to get out of the location before it is destroyed. NER.GAL was off with his space chariot. NIN.URTA was temporarily held back by his father EN.LIL. The specific instructions to warn his fellow Earthling Ibru-Um or Abram about the imminent attack was handed out from EN.LIL for his son.

After he had arrived at the spot where there were Weapons of Terror were hidden, NIN.URTA for NER.GAL already began the ME's to wake the weapons that were asleep. When they were woken, NER.GAL assigned them task names:

* One Without Rival

* Blazing Flame

* One Who With Terror Crumbles

* Mountain Melter

* Wind That The Rim Of The World Seeks

* One Who Above And Below No One Spares

* Vaporizer Of Living Things

If the timing was correct, EN.LIL gave the signal to NIN.URTA and

NER.GAL to start. They headed towards Mount Masha in the heart of the Fourth Region. The weapon that was first set in motion by NIN.URTA. It pounded the top of Mount Masha and slicing it away, and the inside of the mountain immediately melted. NIN.URTA was then able to explode the following weapon, which was located above the Place of the Celestial Chariots. The blast's impact shook the Earth. In the Place of the Celestial Chariots was leveled instantly. The forest surrounding the plain were flattened due to the explosion.

NER.GAL Not wanting to lose, ERRA the Annihilator was able to fly over the five cities and destroyed each of them using a weapon of terror. The inhabitants of the city, who NABU were in the process of joining the military of his father's immediately went extinct. The surrounding mountains became a slurry of dust, and the waters of the ocean poured in to blend with the remains of cities.

NIN.URTA and NERGAL after having expended their energies, as well as Weapons of Terror, came to rest, and looked at the destruction they caused on the city and its surroundings in the Fourth Region. They were however perplexed by what was emerging out of the ruined plain. The dark cloud began to rise in the middle of it, and there was an Evil Wind. The storm continued to increase in the course of the day until it blocked out sunlight as it was dark and the edges of the cloud glowed in a way that hinted at death.

Two cousins in desperate need of calling on their fathers to inform them they were in danger. Evil Wind was heading toward the First Region, and that it would not be stopped. EN.LIL and ENKI were then able to sent the word to Anunnaki. Anunnaki.

The Evil Wind (i.e. radioactive cloud) moved north and eastward towards the valleys of the Tigris and Euphrates rivers, traveling between Eridu to Sippar and Sippar, killing all living organisms within its path. It also laid an ashlod over the earth. The river became poisonous, and the soil was dry. Both animals and people died. The famed Sumerian Civilization, the first to be discovered, was destroyed.

In all the cities of the First Region, only Babili or Babylon which was the place where MAR.DUK was able to establish his home, was not spared. This is an incident which EN.KI as well as EN.LIL believed to be a sign that MAR.DUK had been destined for be the most powerful of all gods/ Anunnaki which he been claiming.

From the Earthlings who were granted the title of king in Sumer Only Ibru-Um / Abram and his descendents survived to carry on the bloodlines that began by Adapu.

Chapter 6: Marduk is the commander of four region

EN.LIL contemplates his past, destiny and fate, and he agrees with Marduk's Supremacy. He decides to move to the lands above the ocean. EN.KI offers his brother EN.LIL goodbye. EN.KI considers the past an indication of the future. When is determined to write down his every moment to a book to be preserved for future generations. He assigns a scribe called Endubasar to record his thoughts. Endubasar scribes the sentences from EN.KI in cuneiform, on 14 tablets made of clay that is wet.

In the meantime, until I know more details about what happened to the Anunnaki in the aftermath of this tragedy, look up Bible Genesis 19 for interactions among the descendants of Abraham as well as the Elohim/Anunnaki.

2200 BC - The Akkadian city Ur passes to the Amorites which, in turn, build cities like Assur, Mari and Babylon.

2,000 bc ~ The Hittites (i.e. Indo-Europeans) conquer Anatolia (i.e. the region that encompasses present-day Turkey) and start to establish their own kingdom in the region. Around 1600 B.C., the Hittites are in control of the area encompassing the northern portion of modern-day Syria.

2200 BC - 2200 BC Bronze Age in Scotland begins. It lasts until 400 B.C.

2200 BC. 2200 BC Sumerian King List is compiled. It consists of fifteen tables. It begins by stating:

"When the kingship was lowered from heaven."

A different older Sumerian text includes the following phrase:

"Kingship had been lowered from heaven... The exalted tiara and the throne of kingship had been lowered from Heaven."

The scholars who been able to translate this text Sumerian King List is translating the book as per their individual belief methods and capabilities. Even with the overwhelming volume of evidence to prove the possibility of its existence, many scientists aren't convinced that Earth could have evolved from a collision between two Planets Nibiru and Tiamat and that the existence on Earth could have come as an outcome of the collision. In the end they are unable to consider the idea of an Nibiru year being equivalent to 3600 Earth years. Therefore, they are unable to accept the length of time in which each of the kings was acknowledged to be ruling. At the end of the day, they reject the source as partially fiction. The text that follows is from the work of Laurence Gardner called Genesis Of The Grail Kings and is also taken from the

Electronic Text Corpus Of Sumerian Literature project.

Primarily derived from the Sumerian Text, which is given the id of W-B/144. The postdiluvian and antediluvian rulers prior to the adappa's reign included:

The kingship was taken down from heaven, the kingship was attained in Eridu(g). The year Eridu(g) AL.LU.LIM was crowned king and ruled for 28800 years. A.LAL.GAR was king for 36,000 years. Two kings ruled over 64,800 years.

After that, Eridu(g) went down and the title of king to Bad-tibira passed. In Bad-tibira EN.MEN.LU.ANNA reigned for 43200 years. In the following years, EN.MEN.GAL.ANNA was in power for 28800 years. After that, DUMU.ZI The shepherd had a reign of 36 years. Three kings ruled for an average of 180,000 years.

When Bad-tibira died, the throne of Larak (variously, Larag) was handed over. In Larak

EN.SIPA.ZI.ANNA (also known as EN.SIPAD.ZID.ANA was king for 28800 years. He was a single king, and was ruled for 28800 years.

In the end, Larak went down and the throne passed to Sippar (variously, Zimbir) was taken. The king of Sippar EN.MEN.DUR.ANNA was king for over 21,000 years. He was a king for two thousand years.

In the following years, Sippar lost his throne and the title of king was transferred to Shuruppak (variously, Curuppag) was transferred. In Shuruppak UBAR.TUTU or UBARA.TUTU was king for 18600 years. A single king was king for 18600 years.

In 5 cities, 8 reigned kings, they were in power throughout 241,200 year. And then the Flood took over the city.

Notice: Despite the fact that the Sumerian King List states it was under the rule of UBAR.TUTU when the Flood took place, and his rule was followed by the reign of GA.UR and GA.UR, different Sumerian sources (and Hebrew tradition) state that it occurred during the time of UBAR.TUTU's son, ZIUSUDRA / UTNAPISHTIM / NOAH and that it was during his reign when the Flood took place.

Following the Flood that had been sweeping over the area and the kingship had been taken down from heaven and the kingship remained at Kish (variously Kic). Then, in Kish, GA.UR / JUCUR was the king. He had a reign of 1,200 years. (For a time -960 years- the Nephilim queen, NIDABA, (variously GULLA.NIDABA.ANNAPAD), reigned in Kish.) Then

KULLASSINA BEL (variously PALAKINATIM) reigned for over 900 years.

Then NANGISH.LISHMA or NANJICLICMA Then NANGISH.LISHMA / NANJICLICMA / NANGISHKUSHMA was in power for 670 years. It lasted 3 months, and three days. Then

EN.TARAH.ANA reigned for 420 year. In the following years, BAHINA and BABUM was in power over 300 years. After that, BU.AN.UM or PUANNUM reigned for 840 year. After that, KALIBUM was ruled for the duration of 960 years. In the following years, QALUMU / KALUMUM / GALUMUM was king for 840 years. After that, ZUQAQIP and ZUKAPIP had a 900-year reign. After that, ATABBA and ATAB and ABA was in power during 600 years.

2000 BC Hurrians are seen all over Syria and

Mesopotamia.

2000 BC Proto-Greeks take over The Peloponnesus (i.e. the present-day islands of south Greece) and established the Minoan civilisation. An important island city belonging to Thera, a major island city of the Minoan civilisation, Thera, will be destroyed when volcanic eruptions of

Santorini volcano at 1450 B.C. The Minoan civilization would flourish for further fifty years up to 1,400 B.C., when its principal home, that is, Crete is ravaged by (Mycenaean) conquerors of mainland.

1900 B.C. Bronze Age flourishes, the megalithic stone site of Stonehenge was built according to estimates of the most common sources.

1,894 BC 1,894 bc. Amorite Dynasty begins at Babylon.

1 800 BC - The Assyrian empire was founded by Shamshi-adad.

1.800 BC Ceremonial centres have been established across Peru throughout the Western Hemisphere.

1,792 to 1,595 B.C. In the reign of the reign of King Hammurabi The kingdom of Babylon thrived in the Old Babylonian Period with the city of Babylon as its capital. Babylon is a region that was formerly occupied by Sumer and Akkad.

1,785-1.570 B.C. 1.785 to 1.570 BC Hyksos is an increase of Asiatic peoples in the Delta region of the Nile is the beginning of the Middle Kingdom of Egypt and ending of the XIIth Dynasty, and heralds the time that is known as the Second Intermediate Period. The Asiatic invaders would eventually subdue to the Egyptians under their rule for as far and as far north as Cusae. The Theban rulers would serve as vassals of the Hyksos rulers up to the time of around 1,567 B.C., when Kamose takes back the lands that lie within the Nile Valley and his brother, Amosis I, recaptures Avaris, the Hyksos capital city of Avaris.

1760-1750 BC - 1,760 to 1,750 bc Hammurabi releases his collection of law, known as known as the Code of Hammurabi. The Code is comprised of 278 laws. It is believed that the Akkadian language was declared the official language of the Empire.

Tribes referred to as Chaldeans were first to enter the Babylonian Empire as well as, by joining with the Babylonians The Chaldean culture came to be synonymous with the Babylonian tradition.

1,760 BC Jacob 1,760 bc Jacob Israel is the one who leads his family and descendents to Egypt.

1.700-1600 B.C. The cities-states of Asia come under the control of the Shang Dynasty.

1.600-1200 B.C. 1200 to 1,200 BC Mycenaean civilization thrives throughout the region covered by modern-day Greece.

1,595 B.C. - The Hittites travel south towards the Euphrates River, which is located in Anatolia and take over Babylon. Babylon. They do not have their control over the city but their plan is in order to take Mesopotamia. The advance of the Hittites is stopped but with the help of Hurrians.

1,595 - 1,155 B.C. In the aftermath of the fall of Babylon The Cassites are a group of people living within the Zagros mountains, take Babylon. They'll hold on to Babylon for almost four centuries. This is a time called the Middle Babylonian Period.

1,567 BC 1,567 BC Hyksos invaders are defeated from the area by Kamose as well as Amosis I. Amosis is the first to be defeated, and the "New Kingdom" is established in Egypt. It would last until 1 990 B.C. This is the time of "warrior-kings," which consist of Amenophis IV/ Akhenaten as well as Tutankhaten and Tutankhamun one of which was a fervent devotee of god Aten and the later of Amun.

1.550-1500 B.C. 1550-1500 BC Aryans were a race of people that came from the Swat Valley that is now that is now Pakistan relocated to the east in an attempt to erase their Indus Valley civilisation. Then they move eastwards to the Ganges and then move southward to control the entire middle of the present-day India.

The Aryans have brought to their one of the oldest religions that are still in existence up to this day: Hinduism. The Hindu faith is founded on the belief that there are numerous gods that are accountable for nature's gifts One god is accountable for the warmth provided by sunlight, a different is responsible for the atmosphere as well as the air. The supreme ruler is Brahma The One Who Exists with the help of Vishnu as the preserver as well as Shiva who is the one who destroys.

1.550 B.C. The city walled by Jericho was toppled. Jericho is destroyed. Hebrew mythology states that Jericho's walls Jericho was destroyed in an troops led by Joshua. Israelite, Joshua (the successor to Moses) however the first date that could be considered to date Joshua being engaged would have been around 1400 B.C. Jericho would then (circa the 9th century B.C.) be rebuilt and even occupied following the Exile of the Israelites (circa 538 B.C.).

1500 BC - The Enuma Elish, the epic Babylonian tale of Creation is composed. The story is later adapted and later by Hebrew scribes in the early chapter of the Book of Genesis for the Hebrew Bible.

1500 BC. 1500 BC Egyptians move further south into the Nubian Desert to take possession of the area that was populated by the Kush up to they reach the Fourth Cataract of the Nile.

1.500-1200 B.C. Kingdom of the Sumerian City-States spawns the Middle Assyrian Empire.

1500-1250 BC 1,500 to 1,250 bc Hebrews remain in bondage in Egypt.

1,450 B.C. The creation of the Vedas in the language of the past of Sanskrit began at the Indus Valley. The Vedas are a hymn to the Hindu faith.

1400-1150 BC - 1,400 to 1,150 bc. New Hittite Empire flourishes in the Mesopotamian region.

1.400 BC - The first type of alphabet was developed in the Phoenicians.

1,400 B.C. Minoan civilization is wiped out by invading tribes who came from mainland Peloponnese, possibly they were the Mycenaeans

1.400 to 1100 BC 1,400 to 1,100 bc. Mycenaean civilization thrives in the area that will eventually become the southern part of Greece.

1,370 - 1,362 B.C. Amenophis IV/ Akhenaten enforces the monotheistic worship of suns on his followers in Egypt.

1,361-1,352 BC Tutankhaten 1352 to 1,352 bc Tutankhaten Tutankhamun is back in Egypt to worship several gods, chief of them was Amun.

1,240 BC - The Jewish religious system, as well as the belief in Jahweh, the monotheistic god (i.e. Jehovah) began by establishing the Covenant of Moses with Yahweh at the time of the exodus of the Israelites to Egypt.

1200 BC - The Hittite empire crumbles.

1200 BC - The Greeks destroyed The city of Troy located in Anatolia.

1200 to 1,200 - 400 BC 1200 to 400 BC - Civilization in terms of the development of social order, commerce and religion, was established in the Western region of the Olmec of the Mexican Gulf Coast, the Zapotec of Monte Alban and the Chavin of Peru. They constructed pyramids like those built within the Nile Valley.

1,166 B.C. Ramesses III, the last famous Egyptian Pharaoh is killed. After his demise, Egypt comes under the authority of Libyan monarchs, who had been at peace with Egypt during the previous few years.

1.100 - 900 B.C. The first Chinese Dictionary of Chinese is written.

1 - 1,010 BC Saul rule in Israel.

1,027 B.C. Shang dynasty from China is toppled by the Chou dynasty.

1100-970 BC David reigns over Israel.

1 - 970 B.C. 1,010 to 970 bc Hebrew alphabet was developed by a combination of the Semitic script.

1000 BC - The tribes of the twelve descendants of Jacob and Israel are joined under the the reign of King David from Judah.

1,000 BC. Early Iron Age in Italy starts.

Between 1000 and 700 B.C. The existence of a group called the Arameans within the area of Assyria is the basis for the Empire that was the Aramean City-States. Their specific language, Aramaic is the primary language that the first Hebrew gospels were first recorded.

From 1,000 up to 300 BC 1000 to 300 BC Phoenicians were a sea-faring group who occupied a territory on the east coast of the Mediterranean Sea, become more settled and these settlements join together in the Empire comprising The Phoenician City-States.

994 BC Teutonic tribes of Central Europe move westward to the Rhine River.

970-930 BC Solomon reigns over Israel.

930 BC - Following the demise of King Solomon The nation of Israel is divided in two parts: Judah located in south including Jerusalem being its capital and Israel in the north and Samaria as the capital city.

After the death of King Solomon His son Rehoboam became the new king of Israel. Northern tribes been loyal to David who had brought them into a united nation. But that feeling of allegiance waned in the Solomon's time. When Solomon was gone, they were no longer interested and decided to stop being members of the united nation.

Based on Scripture, the Hebrew Bible in the book of I Kings, chapter 12 Verse 16:

In the end, when the entire nation of Israel noticed that the King refused to listen to them and the people questioned the king: "What percentage do we share in David? We do not have any inheritance from the child of Jesse. To your tents, O Israel! Now, look at your house, O David'.

In 900 B.C., the Kush region Kush splits off from Egypt and becomes an autonomous kingdom. The Kushites are a black-skinned Nubians who lived peacefully with Egyptians and their northern neighbours as well as conqueror over the centuries, and who eventually want to be independent.

810 BC: Phoenician maritime traders build Carthage as a city. Carthage located on the northern shores of Africa within the area that would later be Tunisia.

800 BC - The author, Homer, composes his two epics: the Iliad as well as the Odyssey.

776 BC The very initial Olympic Games are held in Greece.

753 BC Rome was founded upon the Tiber River, which flows through Italy.

775 BC The year 750 BC saw the Kush begin to defeat Egypt.

747-539 BC 747-539 BC Kingdom of Babylon is a part of in the Neo-Babylonian Period.

721 BC - The kingdom of Israel is conquered by Assyrians. The Jews are scattered throughout the Mediterranean globe.

661-332 BC 661 to 332 bc Late Dynastic Period arises in Egypt

Around 650 B.C. Iron Age in China begins.

From 610 to 560 BC 560 BC - The Anunnaki begin to depart from the Earth in their home at the Nazca Spaceport.

609 BC. Assyrian Empire collapses.

605-520 BC The founding father of Taoism Lao-Tse is alive in this time.

604 BC King Nebuchadnezzar II takes the Kingship of Babylon.

601 BC - The kingdom of Judah is transformed into a state of vassal that is transferred to Babylon.

587 bc. - The Kingdom of Judah passes to Babylon. Babylonians.

586 BC - The first book in the Hebrew Bible are written.

581 BC - King Nebuchadnezzar II conquers Palestine and is burned to the ground in Jerusalem.

563-483 B.C. Siddhartha, the religious leader Gautama, the founder of Buddhism lived throughout this time.

559-331 B.C. Cyrus the Great (559 - 559 -) governs the Persian Empire in the wake of his deposing of the king Nabonidus. Cyrus will be ruled by the strict direction from Darius I (522 - 486), Xerxes (485 - 465) and Artaxerxes (465 465 - 424). The decree that was issued by the King Cyrus the Great in 538 B.C., that the Temple of the Jews in Jerusalem was rebuilt.

551 BC - The sage, Confucius is born.

555 BC - Arabs begin crossing through Red Sea to settle throughout Ethiopia.

539 BC. Greeks beat Carthage.

539 BC. Persian Empire conquers Babylon.

537-445 bc 537-445 bc Israelites come back to Judah for a second time to join in one country.

509 B.C. - Roman Republic is established. The Etruscan people who originally resided on the Tiber River, on the peninsula later called Italy was subjugated and exiled by the newly established Roman civilization.

500 B.C. Adena civilization flourishes across The North American Continent in the area that later became called The Ohio River Valley.

490 BC - 490 BC Battle of Marathon results in the defeat of the Persians at the at the hands of the Athenians as well as the conclusion in the First Persian War.

431-404 bc. 431 to 404 bc. Great Peloponnesian War takes place between the Greek city-states of Athens and Sparta.

From 305 to 51 BC The Ptolemaic Dynasty started during the rule of Ptolemy I from 305 to 282.

282 bc. Roman Empire, which had begun as a loose confederation cities-states, is successful in taking over or in absorbing surrounding tribes, till the entirety part of the Italian peninsula becomes unification.

241 BC. Carthaginians who reside on Sicily's island Sicily are wiped out at the hands of Romans.

200 BC Carthage is destroyed in 202 BC by Romans.

160 BC Macedonian Greece is taken over by the Roman Empire, which now encompasses completely the Mediterranean Sea.

100 B.C. The first books from the Old Testament of the Hebrew Bible is complete.

From 61 until 49 BC From 61 to 49 BC Roman Army under Roman Emperor Julius Caesar, conquers Spain and Gaul.

Chapter 7: Enuma Elish (The Babylonian Epic of Creation)

Tablet I

1. When the heavens above were not there,

2 Earth beneath the earth was not yet in existence ---

3 Then there was Apsu The first of their line, and their heir,

4. And the demiurge Tiamat who was the mother of the entire group;

5 They mixed their waters

6 Prior to meadowland coalescing, and the reed-bed had to be discovered ---

7 And not one of the gods had created

8 Or came to be, even though there was no decree of destiny,

9 Gods were made inside them:

10. Lah(mu and Lah(amu was formed, and they were born.

11 As they grew and gained in the size of their bodies.

12. Ansar and Kisar both of whom excelled were created.

13 They extended their lives and multiplied their lives.

14 Anu 14 Anu, their son may be as successful as his father.

15 Anu The son beat Ansar,

16 Then Anu had a child with Nudimmud who was the son of Nudimmud.

17 Nudimmud was a champion of his parents:

18 Exceptionally discerning, mindful and strong;

19 Stronger than the father's son, Ansar

20 He did not have a rival in the realm of gods. His brothers.

21 The holy brothers gathered together

22 The rumbling of their voices became intense, and Tia-mat was thrown into chaos.

23 They slammed the nerves of Tia-mat

24 In their dance they sparked alarm throughout Anduruna.

25 Apsu didn't diminish the clamour of their supporters,

26 And Tia-mat did not speak in the face of the two.

27 Their behavior was displeasing her

28 Despite the fact that their behavior wasn't ideal the woman wished they could be spared her children.

29 Then Apsu is the god-begetter of the gods of heaven,

30 Calls Mummu the vizier of his, and addressed him.

31 "Vizier Mummu, who gratifies me with pleasure

32 Come, let us go to Tia-mat!"

33 They left and sat with Tia-mat in front,

34 They gathered around gods and their daughters.

35 Apsu open his mouth

36, and Tia-mat is addressed as Tia-mat

37 "Their actions have become distasteful for me.

38 I am unable to do anything but rest throughout the day, or rest in the midnight.

39 I'm going to smash and tear down the way they live

40 Silence may rule and we could fall asleep."

After Tia-mat had heard this, she was elated.

42 She was angry and wept at her husband,

43 She wept in pain she was angry within herself.

44 She was deeply grieved by the (plotted) terrible,

45 "How do we demolish the things we've created?

Their behavior creates distress, we should take care to discipline them gently."

47 Mummu came forward in the presence of the counsel of Apsu-Apsu-

48 (As from) an agitated vizier remained in the direction of his Mummu-(As from)

49 "Destroy my father's property this lawless manner of living,

50 So that you can take a rest during the day and rest at midnight!"

51 Apsu was delighted with himself, and his smile was beaming

52 For he'd plotted wickedly against the gods his children.

53 Mummu placed both arms over Apsu's neck.

54 He was on his knees and kissed him.

55 What did they plan at their gathering

56 It was told to gods by their Sons.

57 The gods heard this and were furious.

They were overwhelmed by silence. They sat silently.

The 59 Ea who is the best in understanding, skillful and well-educated,

60 Ea, who is aware of all about everything, spotted their tricks.

It was a design that he conceived and developed it into universal,

The 62-year-old masterfully executed the incantation with aplomb, his simple Incantation.

64 He read it out loud and placed it upon the sea,

64 He was a slumbering king. his body as he slept deep.

65 He laid Apsu to bed in the midst of a long night,

65 And Mummu counsellor was anguished and agitated.

The 67-year-old split (Apsu's) sinews. tore off his crown

The 68-year-old swept away his aura and placed the blame on himself.

The 69-year-old bound Apsu and then killed him.

70 Mummu He was kept in a cage and was handled rough.

The 71-year-old set up his home on Apsu,

72 and firmly held onto Mummu while he held the noserope in his hands.

After Ea was bound and killed his foes,

He had won against the foes of his,

75 He lay peacefully in his room,

He called it Apsu the god of his shrine, which were ordained by him.

In the following year, he built the living quarters of his home within it.

The 78th and Ea as well as Damkina the wife of Damkina have sat admirably.

The chamber of destinies, in the chamber of archetypes

80 The most wise of the smart, the wise gods' sage Be-l was created.

1981 In Apsu Was Marduk born.

In pure Apsu is Marduk born.

His father was 83 years old, and he was his father,

85 Damkina his mother gave Damkina 84. His mother bore him.

85 He washed into the breasts of gods

The nurse came up to her and made him feel fear.

The shape of his face was nicely built, his eyes were sharp and his eyes was captivating,

The growth of his body was masculine He was strong at the very beginning.

89 Anu was his father's child was there,

90 He exulted and smiled, his heart was full of joy.

1991 Anu was perfect in his work The beauty of his soul was amazing,

He also became extremely impressive, achieving the highest levels in all his qualities.

The members of his group were amazing,

Uncapable of grasping with the mind, it is difficult even to see.

95 Four of his eyes and four ears.

The flame erupted while he licked his lips.

The ears of his four children grew in size,

93 His eyes also were open to everything.

99 His height was high and larger than the gods.

100 His legs were more than the limits of his body, and his character was more powerful.

101 ' Mari -utu, Mari-utu,

The Son The Sun God and the sun god of gods.'

The 103-year-old was adorned with the power of Ten Gods, so exalted was his strength.

The Fifty Dreads had been placed on him.

105 Anu was formed, and was the birthplace of the four winds

They were given to him "My son, let them whirl!"

The dust he created was 107. He made a hurricane to propel it.

A wave was made by 108 to cause a stir to Tia-mat.

109 Tia-mat was lost; the night and day she was in a panic.

110 Gods did not time off, and they . . . .

In their thoughts, they formulated evil plans,

112 They also they addressed their mother Tia-mat

112 "When Apsu, your spouse was killed,

114 You did not stand to his side, but did not move. You sat in silence.

115 Four terrible wind gusts have been created

We are here to throw the reader into confusion and then we're unable to rest.

117 You didn't give a second thought to Apsu and your wife,

113 Not even Mummu, who is in prison. You are now on your own.

From now on, you'll be in consternation!

120 As to us, you cannot relax, don't have love for us!

We must ponder our burdens. our eyes are empty.

122 Take the yoke that is immovable to allow us to be able to sleep.

Create a battle, take revenge them!

124 [. .] . . . . It will be reduced to nil!

The 125 Tia-mat listened to, and she was pleased by the message,

"126" (She told her,) "Let us make demons, [as you] have advised."

The gods gathered inside her.

128 They thought of evil against gods, their childbearing partners.

129 They . . . . . And took the side of Tia-mat

130 Hardly plotting the future, he is agitated by night and daytime,

130 lusting for war and raging, storming

132 They created an event to create conflicts.

133 Mother H(ubur Who is the source of all things,

The 134 possessed irresistible weapons and created giant serpents .

135 They had sharp teeth. they were ruthless . . . .

By using poison instead of blood she was filling the bodies of those who died.

She clad the frightful monsters in dread.

The 138 she infused them with a radiance and created them to be godlike.

140 (She stated,) "Let their onlooker faint,

140"Hope they continue to jump forward and never stop."

141 She invented the Hydra and the Dragon The hairy Hero

142 The Great Demon, the Savage Dog, and the Scorpion-man,

The 143 demons with the most ferocious attacks, the Fish-man, as well as the Bull-man

The 144 armored vehicles are awe-inspiring and awe-inspiring weapons when it comes to battle.

145 Her orders were mighty that they were not to be disregarded.

In all, she produced eleven such.

The gods were 147 among them as well as her sons. they were her hosts,

The 148-year-old lifted Qingu as she magnified Qingu among the others.

The direction of the army and the instructions of the host

150 Weapons bearing and campaigning, as well as the mobilisation of conflicts,

151 The supreme executive power of war, the supreme command

He was entrusted with 152 and set him upon a the throne.

150 "I have performed the spell on you and elevated you to the realm of the gods.

In 154, I've handed you the rules for all gods.

The 155th person you have exalted is indeed awe-inspiring by my wife, and You are well-known,

Your commands should be the prevailing force over all Anunnaki."

He was presented with her Tablet of Destinies and fastened it to his breasts,

It's 158 (Saying) "Your order may not be changed; let the utterance of your mouth be firm."

159 Following Qingu was elevated and obtained the ability of Anuship,

160 He set the fates for gods, her sons

161 "May your lips subdue the god of fire,

162 You may let your poison, through the accumulation of it put down the aggression."

Tablet II

1 Tia-mat brought together her designs

2. A battle organized against gods and her children.

3 From now on, Tia-mat has plotted to commit to commit evil due to Apsu

4 It was revealed to Ea that she had planned the war.

5 Ea was the one who heard about this issue,

6 He was silent inside his room and lay in a slumber.

7 When he'd been reflecting and he had his anger diminished

8 He commanded his steps towards Ansar his father.

9 He was in the presence of his father's child, Ansar,

10. And was connected to his plotting with Tia-mat.

11 "My father's name is Tia-mat, and our mother has developed an aversion to us

12 She has created the hostage in her wild anger.

13 The gods of all the world are turning to her

14 Even the ones who you (pl.) have conceived, also join her side

15 They . . . . . And took the slant of Tia-mat

16 As if a madman plotting and unresting at night and during the day

17 Tempted to fight and raging, storming

18 They created a gathering in order to create conflict.

19 Mother H(ubur Who is the one who shapes everything

20 Alluding irresistible weapons and was the birthplace of giant serpents.

21 These had sharp teeth. they were brutal.

22 Instead of blood, she drained the bodies of those who died.

23 She covered the terrifying creatures with fear,

24 She gave them an aura, and they became Godlike.

25 (She stated,) "Let their onlooker be a sluggish death,

26 May, they continuously move forward, and they never stop."

27 She invented the Hydra and the Dragon and the Hairy Hero,

28 The Great Demon, the Savage Dog, and the Scorpion-man,

29 demons fierce, including the Fish-man, as well as the Bull-man

30 vehicles of unstoppable weapons that are unflinching in the fight.

31 Her orders were mighty that could not be denied.

32 In all, she created eleven such items.

33 In the presence of Gods and her children who she made her hosts,

34 She lifted up Qingu and praised him in front of the others.

35 The leader of the army instructions of the host

36 Weapons' use and the campaigning process, as well as the mobilisation of war,

37 The executive power of battle supreme command

38 She gave him the throne the throne and seated him on seat on a throne.

39 "I am casting the spell to you and placed you to the throne of gods.

40 I've handed over to you the law of all gods.

41 You truly are elevated, my wife You are well-known,

42 Allow your orders to triumph over the Anunnaki."

43 She handed him tablets of Destinies and sewed it on his breasts,

44 (Saying) "Your order may not have changed; let the utterance of your mouth be firm."

45 after Qingu was elevated, she had gained the ability of Anuship

46 He set the fates of the gods. her sons

47 "May the words you speak out with your lips subdue the god of fire,

48. May you poison your body by its accumulation be the cause of your the aggression."

49 Ansar hearings; the issue was deeply alarming.

50 He shouted "Woe!" and took a bite of his lip.

51 The heart of the man was turmoil, and his thoughts couldn't be soothed.

52 Over Ea was his son's cry was a bit tepid.

53 "My Son, you are the one who started the war,

54 You are responsible for the actions you and only you did!

55 You set off and defeated Apsu,

56 And to Tia-mat, who you have threw into a rage, what are her kin?"

57 The gathering of counsel The prince of wisdom,

The wisdom-creator Nudimmud is the god who created wisdom.

With soft words and soothing utterances

60 He was kindly answered by his father Ansar

"61 "My father is a deep-mind and destiny-maker,

Who holds the power to create or destroy

64 Ansar the deep-mind that decides fate,

64 Who is the one with the ability to create as well as to demolish,

65 I would like to tell you something I want you to calm down to a minute

Remember the fact that I have done a positive action.

After I killed Apsu

Anyone who could have seen the situation as it is now?

69 Then I swiftly got him out of the way

70 What for me to kill him?"

70 Ansar saw the words that pleased his heart.

72 He felt his heart swelled and he was able to talk to Ea.

72 "My my son, your acts fit for the status of a god,

74 You're powerful enough to deliver an unrivalled punch . . [. . .]

75 Ea. Your deeds fit for the status of the gods,

The 76th person you can hit is strong enough to take an unrivalled punch . . [. . .]

77 Get in front of Tia-mat to calm her,

78 . . [. . .] . . . she will rage at the prayer."

He heard the address from Ansar his father.

80 He followed the road to her and then continued along the way to get there.

When he left, He was aware of Tia-mat's tricks,

The 82-year-old stopped then sat in silence, before he was turned around.

The 83-year-old entered the the august Ansar

He addressed him in a smug manner,

85 "[My father's] Tia-mat's actions are just far too great for me.

I saw her plan her incantation, but my own wasn't quite as good (to that).

The strength of her is immense and she's overflowing with fear.

Her overall strength is powerful, no one will be able to go against her.

89 Her incredibly exaggerated cry didn't diminish,

90 [I was afraidof her scream and walked away.

My father, keep fighting Send a third person to the.

Although a woman's strength is tremendous however, she isn't equal with the masculine strength.

93 Break up her group and break up her plans

"94 before she places her arms on us."

95 Ansar exclaimed in a rage of anger,

96 Addressing Anu the son of his,

97 "Honoured son, hero, warrior,

The strength of 98 is formidable with an attack that is indestructible

99 Hasten. Stand before Tia-mat

100 Conciliate her anger to allow her heart to calm

101 If she fails to speak to you,

102 Address her to her word of petition to be redeemed."

The 103-year-old heard the address by Ansar his father.

104 He traveled towards her and continued on the way to.

When 105 Anu left, He was aware of the tricks Tia-mat.

The man stopped, fell in silence, and then he turned his back.

He was in into the realm of Ansar the father of his children. his son,

The Penitentiously addressed him.

109 "My father's deeds, Tia-mat's" are just far too much for me.

110 I saw her plan however, my incantation was not equal (to the one she had).

Her strength is powerful She is full of dread

112 She's all-around robust, nobody [can] be able to stop her112 She is a formidable opponent to anyone.

The loud volume doesn't diminish

114 I was scared of her voice and turned away.

115 Do not give up hope. Send an additional person to challenge her.

Although a woman's strength is tremendous but it's not comparable to the masculine strength.

Disband her group and break into her schemes,

118. Before she puts her hands upon us."

119 Ansar fell silent looking at the floor,

120 He nodded at Ea and shook his head.

121 The Igigi as well as all the Anunnaki had gathered.

The 122 sat in a the silence of a tight-lipped mouth.

123 God is not going to face to meet . . [. .]

I would like to see 124 go against Tia-mat . . . . [. .]

But the Lord Ansar was the godfather of the gods who are great,

The 126 was furious at his own heart and didn't summon anyone.

127 A strong son, who is the avenger of his father

128 He is the one who is eager to go to go to war, the soldier Marduk

The 129 Ea called (him) into his personal chamber

130 Explain to him the plans of his.

130 "Marduk Do not be a tyrant and listen at your dad.

132 You are my son that gives me joy,

The 133 adored ones should stand in front of Ansar,

Talk, stand up. posture, smile and reassure him with your gaze."

135 Be-l delighted at the words of his father.

136 He approached and was in the company of Ansar.

The 137 Ansar was there, and his heart was filled with joy,

The man smiled and shook off the fear.

140 "My [father] don't rest in peace. be loud,

140 I'm going to go and meet your needs!

140 [Ansar]: Do not slumber instead, speak up,

I'll be there to meet your needs!

What man has prepared his battle range against you?

Then will Tia-mat whom is a woman strike your with (her) guns?

140 ["My father," begetter Be joyful and rejoice,

You'll soon be walking over the shoulders of Tia-mat!

The number 147 is a begetter Be joyful and rejoice,

Soon, you'll be walking over the neck of Tia-mat!

150 ["Go to my son, awe-inspiring with every knowledge

150 Tia-mat Appeasement with the pure magic of.

150 Drive the chariot of the storm without delay,

and with . .] and cannot be stopped, to turn back."

Be-l smiled over his father's words.

He was elated and spoke to his father.

155 "Lord of the gods," Destiny of the gods"

If I were to be your avenger

If I were to bind Tia-mat to you and keep it,

The assembly should be gathered and announce for me an eminent fate.

159 Sit all of you sitting in Upsukkinakku filled with joy.

160 Let me, through my words make destinies for you.

161 The ideas I make cannot be altered,

162 My command cannot be void or modified."

Tablet III

1. Ansar was able to open his mouth.

2. He the vizier addressed Kaka the vizier of his,

3 "Vizier Kaka, who gratifies my joy,

4. I'll send it the addresses of Lah(mu as well as Lah(amu.

5 You're proficient in asking questions, you have learned about your address.

6 Who are the gods? my fathers, been brought into my throne.

7 Let the gods come to the altar,

8 Let them discuss while they are at a table.

9 They should eat grains as well as consume ale,

10 Let them determine the fate of Marduk and their assassin.

11 Get out, leave, Kaka, stand before them

12 Repetition to all of them what I have told you:

13 "Ansar Your son is sending me,

14 And I'm going to describe his plan.

15-52 = I,11*-48 (* in place of "My father', substitute "Thus,")

53 I called Anu the number 53, but he did not stand up to her.

54 Nudimmud got scared, and then took a break and.

55 Marduk The sage of gods, the son of your god has risen,

56 He is been determined to meet with Tia-mat.

The 57-year-old has been talking to me and has told me,

The number 58-64 is II. It's 156*-162 (* start by quoting: "If)

65 Quickly, right now decide your fate to him immediately,

For him to be able to confront your formidable opponent."

67 Kaka went. He supervised his steps

The 68th day of the month is Lah(mu and Lah(amu The gods of his parents.

He sat down before the ground, kissing it in front of them.

70 He arose in the morning, and said to them He stood up,

71-124 = II, 13-66

The 125th time Lah(h(a and Lah(amu saw their names, they began to cry loudly.

The entire Igigi moaning in dismay,

127 "What did go wrong when she took this deliberation on us?

128 We were not aware of the activities of Tia-mat."

129 All the gods that decide destinies

130 gathered while they walked,

130 They entered Ansar's presence Ansar and were awestruck joy,

The two kissed while they . [. .] within the assembly.

The group sat and talked when they sat down at tables,

They ate grains They also drank ale.

135 They strain the sweet drink through straws

When they had a glass of beer and felt great,

They relaxed Their moods were jolly,

They also decided the destiny of Marduk the avenging of their leader.

Tablet IV

1 They set up a lordly dais to him

2 Then he sat down at his place in front of his parents to be crowned King.

3. (They told them,) "You are the most revered of all the gods,"

4. Your fate is unmatched Your command is similar to Anu's.

5 Marduk 5 Marduk, you're honored by the gods of the highest rank,

6 Your future is unparalleled Your command is similar to Anu's.

7. From now on, your purchase cannot be cancelled.

8 It's your control to elevate and denigrate.

9 The words you speak are certain and your orders cannot be disregarded,

10 No gods can cross the lines you draw.

11 Shrines for all Gods' needs of provisioning

12 You may find out where their sacred places are.

13 We are Marduk Our avenger

14 We have granted you the kingship of the whole of the entire universe.

15 Sit down in the midst of the gathering, allow your word to be exalted,

16 Make sure that your weapons do not be a mishap and may they be able to kill your adversaries.

17 Be-l: spare anyone who is trusting in you.

18 Then destroy God that set his thoughts on the evil."

19 They erected a configuration at the center

20 He addressed Marduk Their son

21 "Your destiny, Be-l is more powerful than the destiny of all gods.

22 Command, and cause destruction and creation.

23 The constellation will disappear when you say it,

24 After a second command, the constellation will reappearate."

25 He issued the order that the constellation dispersed,

26 After a command from the next, the constellation was born in a second time.

27 And when the gods, the fathers of his Gods, were able to see (the result of) his words,

28 They were elated and gave the following congratulation: "Marduk is the king!"

29 He was adorned with an ax, a an throne, as well as an iron rod.

30 They handed him an unstoppable weapon to overwhelm any foe

31 (They stated,) "Go, cut the throat of Tia-mat.

32 Let the wind take her blood to deliver the message."

33 Gods the fathers of his sons set the course of Be-l.

34 Then set him down the path, which is the route of success and prosperity.

35 He made the bow, and made it into a weapon.

36 He put an bow in its place and tied the bow string in.

37 He picked up the club and placed the club in his left hand.

38 His quiver and bow stood at his sides.

39 He set lightning in front of his face,

40 He engulfed his body with flames and tongues.

41 He devised his own net, which encased the Tia-mat's entrails,

42 and stationed the four winds, which were not an element in her escape.

43 The South Wind, the North Wind, the East Wind, the West Wind,

44 He threw it on his net that was tossed by his father Anu.

45 He invented his own version of the Evil Wind, the Dust Storm, Tempest,

46 The Four-fold Wind, the Seven-fold Wind, the Chaos-spreading Wind, the . . . . .Wind.

47 He sounded the seven winds were crafted by him,

48 Then they stood behind them to attack Tia-mat's insecurities.

49 Be-L picked up the Storm-flood as his most powerful weapon.

50 He rode in the terrorizing Chariot of the fantastic storm.

51 He tied four steeds to it, and tied the steeds to it.

52 The Destroyer, The Merciless, The Trampler, The Fleet.

53 Their lips split by their teeth, and they emitted the venom of a snake,

54 They had no experience with fatigue, and were taught to sweep forward.

55 To his left the soldier positioned himself to watch raging battles and a war,

56 On the left conflicts that overwhelm a combat array.

57 He was clad with the tunic, which was a terrifying coat of mail.

On his head, he was wearing an ominous aura.

59 Be-l continued and went to go on his way.

60 He threw his head towards Tia-mat's raging rage.

The lips of 61 was able to hold a spell.

He grasped a plant with his fingers,

Then they milled about him. The gods came around him.

64 Gods, as well as his fathers, mingled around him. Gods came all around him.

65 Be-l was nearer and surveyed the face of Tia-mat.

66 He was observant of the tricks performed by Qingu and her husband.